THE ART OF ENGLISH COMMUNICATION: A PRACTICAL APPROACH

Jayanthi Rajendran, V. Jeya Santhi,
B. Nagalakshmi

INDIA • SINGAPORE • MALAYSIA

ISBN 979-8-89961-486-6

Contents

UNIT-IV: COMMUNICATIVE ENGLISH II 129

Acknowledgment

We, the authors of "The Art of English Communication: A Practical Approach" wish to express our heartfelt gratitude for the collective effort that has brought this book to fruition. This collaborative endeavour allowed us to pool our knowledge and experiences in language, culture, and communication, resulting in a comprehensive resource for learners and educators alike. We extend our appreciation to our colleagues, institutions and publisher for their unwavering support, and we hope that this book serves as a valuable guide in the pursuit of effective communication. We acknowledge our roles in this project, as well as our shared commitment to the advancement of Communication in English. We thank our families and friends for their unwavering support, understanding, and patience throughout this journey, which has been a constant source of strength.

Dr. Jayanthi Rajendran M.A.,M.Phil.,PhD., TEFL
Associate Professor and HOD- Department of English
SRM Easwari Engineering College
Chennai

Dr. V. Jeya Santhi, M.A., M.Phil., B.Ed., PGDELT., Ph.D., PGCTE.
Associate Professor
Department of English
New Prince Shri Bhavani College of Engineering and Technology, Chennai.

Dr. B. Nagalakshmi, M.A., M.Phil., Ph.D., PGDTE.
Assistant Professor
Department of English
SDNB Vaishnav College for Women, Chennai.

Preface

The importance of effective communication in today's interconnected world cannot be overstated. As professors deeply engaged in the fields of language, culture, and communication, we have witnessed the transformative power of language and its ability to bridge cultural divides and foster understanding.

This book "The Art of English Communication: A Practical Approach" represents our collective effort to share our expertise, knowledge, and passion for the subject with students, educators, and all those seeking to enhance their communication skills. With diverse backgrounds in linguistics, cultural studies, and pedagogy, we bring a range of perspectives and experiences to the study of Communication in English.

Our motivation for writing this book stems from a shared commitment to providing a comprehensive resource that guides readers through the intricacies of effective communication in English. We have drawn from our experiences working with students and engaging with the evolving landscape of language and culture to develop a book that covers a wide array of topics on LSRW skills.

We have designed this book to be accessible to a wide audience, from students pursuing degrees in communication to professionals seeking to improve their language skills in a global context. The content is structured to provide both foundational knowledge and practical applications, with exercises and examples that encourage active learning and skill development.

Our approach to this book is founded on the belief that effective communication is not just a skill but a lifelong journey. We hope that the knowledge and insights shared within these pages will empower readers to bridge linguistic gaps and fostering meaningful connections and understanding in a world that continues to grow more interconnected.

As authors, our collective vision for this book is to inspire a new generation of effective communicators, equipped with the tools they need to navigate an increasingly globalized world. We hope that "The Art of English Communication: A Practical Approach" becomes a trusted companion in your journey toward mastering the art of communication.

We would like to extend our deepest thanks to all those who have supported us in this endeavour, from our colleagues, our students, our families and friends. Their unwavering support has been the driving force behind the completion of this book.

Sincerely,
Dr. Jayanthi Rajendran, HOD
SRM Easwari Engineering College,
Ramapuram, Chennai.

Dr. V. Jeya Santhi, M.A., M.Phil., B.Ed., PGDELT., Ph.D., PGCTE.
Associate Professor
Department of English
New Prince Shri Bhavani College of Engineering and Technology, Chennai.

Dr. B. Nagalakshmi, M.A., M.Phil., Ph.D., PGDTE.
Assistant Professor
Department of English
SDNB Vaishnav College for Women, Chennai.

Foreword

There is an ever-increasing need to use English language in day-to-day life. From business to travel to leisure, English makes life easy and helps a person stay connected. It offers 'space' and 'distinctiveness' to every language user in the communicative realm. English comes with its own scope, its own soul. The evolution of English language is organic.

A textbook on English language learning by non-natives is a remarkable milestone indeed. ESL students are confronted with practical challenges, but one has to adopt a systemic approach to learning a new language. A learner should be able to see beyond the superficial, commercial strings in English. There is a fundamental element of beauty attached to English. This pristine trait made English language spread its wings across the world. Thus, learning should happen in its entirety to obtain wholesome results.

The sample exercises, textual references are meant to hone one's productive skills. The authors have considered the various elements involved in the process of learning. The book offers immense scope for better speaking, exposes the readers to plenty of learning aids. Thus, by tapping the components in the book, one can find visibility in the public space. Beyond its ability to help reader gain linguistic dexterity, the book provides space to foster love for a new language.

The exercises given are carefully-chosen, examples tailor-made for learners of different levels. Almost, in a first, this text contains internet references for further study. The colourful, pictorial representations will aid any learner towards better learning outcomes, more so on the grey areas of grammar.

Yet another significance of the book is the element of contemporaneity. Certain components are most relevant and contemporary that include elements of online learning. Multiple strategies offered to every learning task is definitely going to be impactful. With film reviews, poem analysis, Ted Talks and conversation cues, this book is a primer on English language studies.

The editors deserve an obligatory appreciation for their knowledge and involvement in creating a text of this higher order. The readers and learners can now unlock for themselves to a world of profound, lasting and experiential learning.

Prof. Dr. V. Immanuel
Former Principal, RJMCC, Dindigul, TN &
Former Professor & Head/English, BIHER, Chennai

Foreword

When teachers produce teaching-learning materials for their own students, it has many advantages and only one disadvantage. The advantages are for learners, and the disadvantage, for those teachers who take the 'unnecessary' risk. Let me elaborate the latter point in one sentence: For those teachers who engage in materials development, it is a time-consuming, hard work; they have to show and prove that their materials are different from those that were in use hitherto.

The advantages for the learners are many: (i) They get culturally familiar materials to read, though the contents may be unfamiliar. (ii) Students can bridge the gap between the new materials with the new methods those teachers had already introduced in the class. That means, they know in the first instance itself, what they are supposed to do with a particular reading passage, or how they are expected to attempt a particular problem-solving task etc. (iii) They get materials, tasks, and activities—including test materials—that take care of their needs, because they are produced by teachers who know their strengths and weaknesses well. (iv) Finally, perhaps most importantly, those materials are expected to escort the learners beyond their final examinations and degree certificates, into the job market since those materials developers are well aware of the different types of entrance tests and interviews for getting placed in various organizations in the public and private sectors such as banks and government departments. A set of course materials produced by an international agency may not be able to cater to the immediate and concrete needs of the college leavers.

The course materials designed by the three experienced teachers seem to have a clear picture of their learners' needs, and interests. Their long-time classroom experience is expected to have supported in doing justice to their new, self-assigned responsibility.

I wish happy self-involved academic sessions to both the learners and teachers.

Dr. P. Bhaskaran Nair
(Former faculty of English at
Pondicherry University)
nairpbhaskaran@gmail.com

Authors' Brief Profile

Dr. Jayanthi Rajendran
M.A., M.Phil., PhD., TEFL

Having graduated from Madras Christian College, she is a proven professional with over 18 years of teaching experience and counselling culturally diverse undergraduate and postgraduate students. She was awarded PhD from the University of Madras in the year 2012. She has work experience for nearly 18 years in India and abroad, driven to inspire students to achieve personal and academic success. She has profound expertise in facilitating Language learning among various levels of learners. She has published books and research papers in Scopus and Web of Science-indexed journals. She has contributed as a resource person for various International Conferences and seminars and has conducted workshops on the Language Enhancement Program. She has also authored 4 books to her credit. She is a trained IELTS and TOEFL professional. She is currently a member of ELTAI and ASRA. Her areas of specialisation include Literature and English Language Teaching.

Dr. V. Jeya Santhi
M.A., M.Phil., B.Ed., PGDELT, Ph.D., PGCTE

Dr. V. Jeya Santhi's academic journey is remarkable, marked by 15 years of dedicated teaching in universities and arts and science colleges. Currently serving as an Associate Professor of English at New Prince Shri Bhavani College of Engineering and Technology, Chennai, her expertise spans English Language Teaching, Comparative Literature, Translation Studies, and Indian Writing in English.

With over 50 publications in esteemed platforms, including books, Scopus-indexed, UGC CARE-listed journals, and other international and national outlets, her contributions to research are noteworthy. She was recognized with the Innovative Researcher Award in 2021 by Shri Paramhans Education and Research Foundation Trust, New Delhi, for her exceptional research project. As an active member and reviewer for several prestigious organizations like ATINER (Greece), British Council, and ELT@I, she exemplifies global academic collaboration. Since 2022, she has been an esteemed Editorial Board Member of *Bodhi Journals*.

A specialist in English Language Teaching, she has inspired students through more than 20 engaging and interactive sessions, showcasing her dedication to education. Her achievements and passion for literature, education, and research make her a distinguished figure in her field.

Dr. B. Nagalaskhmi

M.A., M. Phil., PhD., PGDTE., PGDJMC

The author holds PhD in ELT (Full-time) from Hindustan University. Completed PGDTE (Distance) from English and Foreign Languages University, Hyderabad. Published 18 articles in Conference Proceedings/ National/ International /UGC CARE Journals, published 5 English Language Teaching Series book and on the Editorial board of ELTIF, an International, Peer reviewed Journal. Member of professional bodies ELTAI, ELTIF, IAFOR and IATEFL. Passionately serving the underprivileged, differently abled through NGOs. With the 12 years of teaching experience capable of motivating and inspiring learners in language learning to achieve exceptional results. Evolving professional skills with constantly updating to the everchanging educational landscape. Currently serving as Assistant Professor in SDNB Vaishnav College for Women.

Unit-1
LISTENING AND SPEAKING

1.1. Introduction

A table can be stable and withstand the weight of the objects placed on it only when all the four legs are of equal in size and mass. If anyone of the legs is shorter or longer than the rest of three, the table may be collapsed. Listening, Speaking, Reading and Writing are similar to the four legs of a table. Lagging behind in anyone of these four skills may fail to produce a good communicator. This book is written by giving equal importance to all the four skills through Integrated approach. Unit 1- Section 1.1 has dealt with developing Speaking and Listening skills in relation to real-life situations such as listening and responding to complaints, listening to problems and offering solutions in both formal and informal contexts. Strategies for Active Listening are given. Classroom practicing activities such as Role play and 'Think-pair-share' are given with examples. The section 1.2 Reading and Writing is designed to give Read aloud practice from a motivational speech followed by comprehension questions to develop Higher Order Thinking skills. This section also deals with Paragraph writing describing the essential components of a good paragraph. This is supplemented with writing a paragraph using proverbial expressions. Section 1.3 emphasizes the need for increasing active vocabulary skills. This includes a creative way of word power building 'Weave a story with vocabulary'. Synonyms and Antonyms are differentiated and a set of five MCQ-type examples for each is given. Last section of Unit 1 deals with Adverbs and Prepositions which are discussed as given in contexts. This includes the types of adverbs with examples and sentence framing using adverbs. Prepositions section deals with forms and functions along with contexts and a mind-map on prepositions of time. All the sections have exercises, individual activities, group activities, classroom practices, tasks, and worksheets and examples based on real-life situations specifically designed to develop Integrated language skills, Higher Order Thinking Skills, Critical and Creative Thinking skills.

1.1.1 Listening and Responding in formal and informal contexts

Read the following transcripts of conversation happening in real-life situations and categorize them as formal and informal.

a)   *Mother (shouts from the kitchen making dosa): "Arun, look at the plate and eat, not the mobile".*

Over a Toll-free call

Customer:)

Automated Voice: If you want to know in Tamil press 1, to know in English press 2, to contact our service staff, press 3.

b)   *In a Language Lab*

Teacher: we are going to conduct listening comprehension today. please log in and put on your headphones and do the activity assigned.

c)   In Airport at a boarding gate

Flamingo Airlines staff: kind attention to the passengers! Boarding for Mangalore flight had started, passengers from seat no 1- 20 can come forward for boarding.

d)   Customer enquiring in a bank

I am not getting any SMS alert for my transactions from the bank for the past one week.

e)   Telephonic Interview

The Interviewer: Can you give a brief on your role and the handled in the previous company?

You all come across these situations in your life. While travelling in a bus, you listen to music. In public places you listen to announcements. In some other contexts, you listen to people over the phone to get some information and facts. In the classroom, you listen to a lecture. While driving you may listen to podcasts. Do you pay the same amount of attention for listening in all these contexts? No, you have varying levels of listening to different contexts. In most of the personal/informal contexts you 'hear' rather than 'listen' whereas in official contexts you sharply listen for some details, facts, data and number, understand verbal and nonverbal cues so as to process for action. This type of listening is known as **'Active listening'**. The following are the techniques involved in **Active listening**.

- Listening to understand rather than to respond

- Paraphrasing and reflecting back what has been said

- Noticing or using non- verbal cues

- Asking open-ended questions to encourage further responses

1. Listening and responding to complaints (Formal Situation)

   Read the following transcript of a telephonic conversation between a customer and a staff of Ultranet broadband company.

   Staff: *Hello, this is Ultranet broadband company. How can I help you?*

   User: *Hi, I am a user of Ultranet broadband. I'm having some problems in my wi-fi access. I want to register a complaint regarding my Internet service.*

   Staff: *I'm sorry to hear that. What has been the problem?*

   User: *My connection has been repeatedly dropping out and when it is connected the speed is very slow.*

   Staff: *Let me check to see if there is a repeated issue with our network in your area. I need your customer ID. Do you, have it?*

   User: *Yes, my subscriber ID is 425-9643.*

   Staff: *Thank you. The system does not show any maintenance in your area.*

   User: *So, the problem must be on my side.*

   Staff: *As I can't say this at this moment, I can send a technician to your home to check this.*

   User: *Ok. At what time and when I can expect him?*

   Staff: *I can get someone out there between 2:00 to 4:00 PM tomorrow. Will someone be at home?*

   User: *Yes, I'll be at home.*

   Staff: *Ok. Our technician will come to your home tomorrow to address this problem.*

   User: *Thank you for taking up my complaint.*

(i) Activity

Practicing listening and speaking through Roleplay – Pair activity

Students can be formed into pairs and take up roles as given below and practice speaking and listening.

1. A customer complaining to a shopkeeper over a billing issue in a supermarket.

2. A customer complaining to the bank manager over some technical issues in accessing his online account.

3. A patient complaining to a dentist over recurring of tooth pain even after treatment.

4. A housewife complaining over replacement of a defective mixer grinder in a home appliances store.

5. A customer complaining to the tailor over inappropriate fitting of his trousers stitched.

2. Listening to problems and offering Solutions (informal)

    There are numerous informal, day-to-day life contexts in which you have to listen to people discussing their problems. You have to listen to their problems, understand the seriousness, and offer solutions. You have to use certain expressions while practicing active listening in informal contexts which demand some solutions to some problems.

    The following activity can be conducted to practice speaking and listening for offering solutions to problems.

1. Classroom Activity

    Think-pair-share

    - *Class size*: any (formed into pairs)

    - *Time frame*: 5-10 minutes

    - *Purpose*: engaged listening, showing empathy, offer solutions

Description: First, students can be formed into pairs. Each pair will have to choose a problem for sharing. One student shares his problem with the other one and the other one has to listen and offer a solution. The problems can be ranging from having an issue of fencing on his farm with his neighbour, a customer getting a defective product, getting stalked over by a stalker or a billing issuing in a supermarket. Finally, each pair has to discuss a problem and offer solutions before the entire class followed by taking turn.

2. Familiarize yourself with the following context of offering solutions to problem.

You are involved in a borrowing from a money lender who started harassing you to give more interest. Write a short paragraph offering a solution to this problem. Your description includes stating the problem, elaboration upon the consequences and offering a solution.

As you stated, I thing you are into a big problem with the moneylender. I can understand your situation that at times of a medical emergency of your family member, you had approached the moneylender who agreed to lend money at rate of 4 %. But later having known about your critical situation and more expenditure, he started demanding 10% of interest. I sympathize with you for being harassed for getting more interest for the money. This is really bad. I think he wanted to exploit you having known about your pathetic situation. It is really bad to know that he is calling you persistently at a time you are shuttling between hospital and home. And I am saddened to hear that he is sending some Gundas to your home. you cannot continue with this type of threatening. What I suggest you is to approach police and seek their support to solve this problem. The money lender may change his ways to you out of fear for police action. This may be a good solution to your problem.

1.2 Reading and Writing

1.2.1. Reading Aloud Practice

Reading aloud is a practice given to create a classroom community by establishing a known text that can be used as the basis for building critical thinking skills that are related and unrelated to reading. This enables the students to construct meanings, connect ideas and experiences across texts, use their prior knowledge, and question unfamiliar words from the text. Reading aloud gives exposure to construct meanings, connect ideas and experiences across texts, use their prior knowledge, and question unfamiliar words from the text. Reading aloud gives students an opportunity to hear the instructor model fluency and exposure to pronunciation aspects of intonation, pay attention to punctuation, and demonstrate meaning embedded in the text.

Listen to this interesting speech given by Ratan Tata.

Motivational Speech by Ratan Tata

"Where did Microsoft, where did Apple, where did Amazon, where did Facebook come from?". It came from where individuals started in garages where ideas were born. Do not grow with a view that something can't be done and so should not be done. How many times have you heard people say 'this can't be done?' It's your job to remove those myths and to get things done. Learn and listen because your whole world is going to be learning and listening. Your success is going to be your humility. In many ways we have been critical of and saddened by What has or has not happened in our country. To a great extent this has been the result of saying 'we can't do this or it can't be done or vested interest'. Things are not done saying these. Ethical practices being thrown to the wind and subjective issues being brought to the table. You in the years ahead are going to be leaders of this country and shaping the destiny of this country. Do not let and do not grow with a view that something can't be done and so should not be done. let me just take a minute and you look at the world around you. Great companies came from ideas that people felt Something could be done and that they could make a difference so as you go out into this world. I would hope that you a would look at being ethical and holding the value systems which you want this country to have. If you think you cannot make a difference, I'd say that you can very well make a difference if you so desire. That you be humble as you look forward. If you speak or sit next to a Nobel laureate, he never tells you that he won a Nobel prize but other people tell you. So let humility be your best defence. And I would say that You always need to take a view that you have had the privilege of a good education. You need to get give back to society some of the learning you have done to do something for your country and for society and you shouldn't merely consider yourself successful based on the prosperity you gain for yourself. But you should go home at night feeling satisfied. If you have made a difference that difference is something each one of us can make. We'll have failures and we've had frustrations but it's a continued commitment that we have to the world around us to ourselves and to the people of India. This is the time that you have used your innovativeness and your creativity and your diligence to complete a curriculum. your real learning starts now as you go into the real world. The tools have been given to you, the experience and exposure have been given to you but what you make in life is what you do after you graduate. There will be thousands of occasions when you have to make difficult decisions. You need to at all times ask yourself if you are doing the right thing and take the decision that's the right thing however difficult or unpopular that may be. Think of yourself as being one of the more fortunate people in this world than that there are millions who are less fortunate and don't ever forget that because you need to look at your life as one where you can make a difference. I am very envious of you coming out into the India of today and tomorrow which is going to be a great country. Play your role and hopefully many of you will be leaders in the in the India of tomorrow. Congratulations once again.

(Source: https://ytscribe.com/v/7m4zQpf3Ouo/)

Answer the following questions:

i.　According to Tata what are the myths that youngsters need to break?

ii.　Individuals started the companies like Microsoft, Apple, Amazon, Facebook in Garage. Analyse and explain this statement.

iii.　How will you imbibe values and ethics in your profession?

iv.　What do you mean by 'give back to the society'?

v.　What have you learnt through your course curriculum?

vi.　What do you understand by this statement?

"Ethical practices being thrown to the wind and subjective issues being brought to the table"

vii.　Synonym of 'humility' is

(a) gratitude (b) insult (c) modesty (d) arrogance

viii.　Antonym of 'diligence' is

(a) industrious (b)ridiculous (c) negligence (d) intelligence

ix.　Refer to an online dictionary and learn the pronunciation of the below given words.

(a) Garage (b) Nobel (c) Laureate (d) Curriculum.

x.　Find out four words from the passage that have long vowel sound. Eg. need, these

1.2.2. Paragraph Writing

1.   Read the following Paragraph and analyse what is wrong with it.

I hate wet and rainy days.

It rained a lot in 1816.... a lot - like every day; the weather in Europe was abnormally wet because it rained in Switzerland on 130 out of the 183 days from April to September. If I was Mary Shelley, I might decide to write a book too. Afterall, it was the only thing you could do without TV or anything. She said that she "passed the summer of 1816 in the environs of Geneva...we occasionally amused ourselves with some German stories of ghosts... These tales excited in us a playful desire of imitation". So, people were stuck inside and bored. Mary Shelley decided to write a book because it was so awful outside. I can totally see her point, you know? I guess I would write a novel if there was nothing else to do.

You may conclude from your analysis that this paragraph has no proper beginning, middle and end and does not convey the meaning in an organized and logical way. Hence this proves to be the best example of bad paragraph. So, you should learn the art of organizing your ideas to write a good paragraph. Remember this analogy while writing a paragraph. You have gone to a hotel and order the food beginning with the starter, main menu and dessert. But if the bearer brings mixing up all these and serves you, 'how would you react?'. You would be disappointed and feeling bad. This is how you are leaving the reader dissatisfied if you are writing an unorganized paragraph. Organizing a good paragraph is an art which you have to master to express your ideas clearly to the readers. You can practice this practice by learning the below given components of paragraph writing.

What are the essential components of a good paragraph?

A good paragraph has an introduction, supportive and conclusive points. The introduction gives the readers an idea about what the paragraph is about. The theme, central idea, characters, setting and statistics can be presented in the introduction. Then the paragraph can be developed into a climax by reaching a crucial point using the supportive points with illustrations and examples. Then all the main points can be deduced to some conclusive points.

A topic sentence is to be used as the main body of ideas. Topic sentence is the nucleus of a paragraph and all other supportive ideas are bound by it. If you are dividing a paragraph into many based on the requirement of length and topic, every paragraph can have a topic sentence. Learn the essential components of a paragraph from the below given figure.

Components of a paragraph

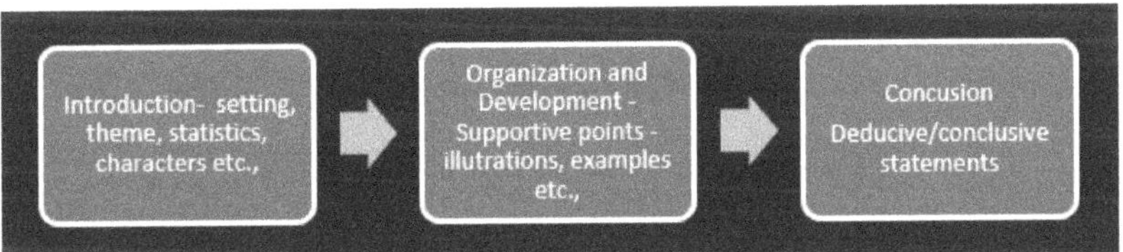

As you have learnt about the structure and organization of paragraph writing, you can learn about writing a paragraph for proverbial expressions from this section.

2. Paragraph Writing using proverbial expressions

According to Mieder, "A proverb is a short, general known sentence of the folk which contains wisdom, truth, morals, and traditional views in a metaphorical, fixed, and memorizable form and which is handed down from generation to generation". It is often metaphorical and use formulaic language. Take for example the proverb 'A stitch in time saves nine'. You know the meaning of 'doing stitching' and 'doing at time'. But you may not get the meaning of the proverb by this type of literal translation of words. It conveys metaphorical meaning. This means any preventive step that one takes at the beginning of a small problem would save him from disastrous consequences.

Examples of Proverbs

Proverbs	Meaning
A friend in need is a friend indeed.	One who helps you at times of difficulty is your real friend.
Actions speak louder than words.	One should bring his thoughts in action rather than speaking about it.
A penny saved is a penny earned.	This gives importance for saving and avoid being a spendthrift. Saving some money is equivalent to earning.
Don't judge a book by its cover	We should not judge anyone from their appearance. They may be ugly but good in their heart.
Honesty is the best policy	Being honest always gives one rewards. One can have many principles and policies in life. But honesty is the best one.
Where there's a will, there's a way.	If you have the determination to do something, however difficult, you can do it.
Don't count your chickens before they hatch.	Life is uncertain. Hence one should not have too much plans about future or of any investments.
Don't put all your eggs in one basket.	This is related to investments. To avoid risk, one should divide and keep his investments in various investment plans.
Too many cooks spoil the broth.	More than required number of people in a work may cause it a failure.
You can lead a horse to water, but you can't make it drink.	You can give guidance or counselling to someone but ultimately, he has to practice and improve upon his own efforts.

6. Guess the proverb from the story below.

    This proverb stresses the fact that one should have a balanced life.

    Too much of work or study without any time for entertainment or other developmental activities will make a person dull and boring. For students, bookish knowledge or academics alone will not help them scale great heights in their career. Overall personality development is very important and for this every person needs to enhance his/her knowledge. The name Jack here is used as a general term to denote a person.

Ravi was a brilliant student who always stood first in his college and won many prizes for academic excellence. He was always seen either in the class or in the library with books in his hand.

Ram was his classmate. Although Ram was not as brilliant as Ravi in terms of scoring marks, he was good at extracurricular activities like quiz, basketball and dramatics.

At the end of the college term many multinational companies visited their college to recruit the best of the students for prestigious jobs in their respective companies. The entire college was very sure that Ravi would bag the most coveted job with a princely salary because of his extraordinary academic performance. But finally, it was Ram who was selected for the best of jobs. Ravi was very angry and demanded an explanation.

The person who conducted the interview told Ravi "It is true that you have better scores. But bookish knowledge alone will not help you perform well in an organization where you have to interact with different people and work as a team player. Ram has better exposure to the world in terms of general knowledge. Moreover, as a sportsman he has learnt the value of sharing and team effort. He therefore has more adaptability and flexibility. We do not want someone who is just brilliant. We want someone who can learn, share and inspire others to perform. This is the reason why we selected him".

There is a valuable lesson to be learnt from this. Every one of us should take time off to equip ourselves with other skills apart from the work we do only then can we make a mark in life.

Your guess is right. The proverb behind this paragraph is 'All work and no play make Jack a dull boy'.

3. Group Activity

    Students can be divided into small groups and each group has to write a Paragraph /story based any proverb of their choice. One student representing the group has to read aloud the paragraph and the rest of the class has to guess the proverb behind it.

4. Journal Writing

    Write a paragraph from the given below proverbs.

    a) Bird in hand is worth two in the bush

    b) The Leopard cannot change his spots

    c) The pen is mightier than the sword

    d) The early bird catches the worm

    e) The grass is greener on the other side of the fence.

1.3. Vocabulary

 Amazing facts about vocabulary

There are roughly 100,000 word families in the English language.

Of all the languages in the world, English has the largest vocabulary of about 800,000 words.

Victor Hugo used an active vocabulary of 38,000 words; Shakespeare, 24,000; and Homer, 8,500. But Horace, with 4,600 words, came significantly below the American journalist, and Xenophon, with 3,200, was about equal to the present-day "average citizen."

According to the Oxford English Dictionary, the longest word in the English language is pneumonoultramicroscopicsilicovolcanoconiosis.

1.3.1 Check your stock of active and passive vocabulary by this small self-assessment activity. Read the following words and frame a sentence using the words.

boutique, enthusiastic, cheerful, admire, hallucination, pathetic, collaborate, irritate, effervescent, humility, flamboyant, boast, plagiarize, resentful, ambiguous, bilateral

If you can recognize all the words, know their meanings and able to frame a sentence, your **active vocabulary** stock is good. If you can recognize most of the words and may not be able to use it in a context by framing a sentence, your **passive vocabulary** stock is more. Educationists believe that using vocabulary in communicative tasks is more beneficial to developing **active vocabulary** than requiring learners to memorize isolated words. You have to increase your stock of **active vocabulary** to improve your proficiency level.

1. Weave a story with vocabulary!

    Learning vocabulary in isolated contexts is very difficult. We learn words by remembering, inferring, associating and guessing while reading from a text in a context. To learn words in a creative way is to randomly take some ten words from a dictionary in a day and write a small story/ paragraph associating them. You can give a title also. The associations can be funny and illogical. The following is an example of this by making associations from a random ten words taken from a dictionary.

band, timid, inquisitive, hospitable, vague, diverse, nutritious, inevitable, desperate, Turkey

Story of a timid Turkey

There lived a **Turkey** which was very **timid.** But it was **inquisitive** and did not want to live in a forest where a **diverse** organism and animals co-exist. It felt life was **vague** and the fellow beings were not **hospitable**. It was **desperate** to go somewhere. It wanted to go and settle in a place where there could be a **band** of music and **nutritious** food.

2.   Task

Take a dictionary/ Thesaurus and choose three or five or ten or as many random words you can take. Learning the meaning and frame sentences by associating them. You can write a paragraph / story.

1.3.2. Synonym and Antonym

Analyse the following sentences in terms of the italicized sentences.

a)   Lasya was *skilled at* playing basketball.

b)   Lasya was *adept* at playing basketball.

c)   The bird *flew away* from the cage.

d)   The bird *escaped* from the cage.

In the sentences a and b replacement of 'skilled' with 'adept' do not change the meaning.

In the sentences c and d replacement of 'flew away' with 'escaped' do not change the meaning. This type of replacing some phrases or words with a single word without changing its meaning is single word substitution. This makes the language crisp and intact. When they are giving same meanings, it is termed as 'Synonyms'. But it can give opposite meanings also. Such words are 'Antonyms' as shown in the below example.

a) He was wearing two *different* colour socks.

b) He was wearing two *same* colour socks.

c) His problem got *alleviated*.

d) His problem got *aggravated*.

In the sentences a and b italicised words are antonyms. In sentences c and d italicized sentences are antonyms.

Worksheet: 1

I   Replace the underlined phrases with a single phrase by choosing from the box given below.

> Determination, emerge, challenges, passion

Deccan Airlines took shape out of his vision and _deep desire for flying high in life. Every chapter of the book gives a feeling of collective thought and will power to get things done in spite of all sorts of difficulties.

II   choose the synonym of the given word from the options given below.

1. Jealous

    a)   envious

    b)   greedy

    c)   lustful

    d)   proud

2. Quest

    a)   trial

    b)   test

    c)   search

    d)   zest

3. Genuine

    a)   Local

    b)   Authentic

    c)   concern

    d)   wise

4. Revenue

    a)   disaster

    b)   return

    c)   regain

    d)   income

5. Foster

    a)   nurture

    b)   safeguard

    c)   protect

    d)   neglect

Key:

1. a)

2. c)

3. b)

4. d)

5. a)

III Choose the antonym of the given word from the options given below.

1. Bestowed

    a)   deprive

    b)   bequeath

    c)   consent

    d)   endow

2. Immense

    a)   humongous

    b)   monumental

    c)   gigantic

    d)   tiny

3. Plunge

    a)   duck

    b)   dive

    c)   rise

    d)   immerse

4. Modest

    a)   unhappy

    b)   impolite

    c)   sullen

    d)   humble

5. Precious

    a)   Expensive

    b)   Rare

    c)   Simple

    d)   cheap

Key:

1. a)

2. d)

3. c)

4. b)

5. d)

1.4. Grammar in Contexts

1.4.1. Adverb

Read the following statements and analyse them in terms of the highlighted words in each sentence.

a) Sanvi speaks **loudly**.

b) This idea is **really** wonderful.

c) My grandfather walks **too** slowly.

In the sentence (a), the highlighted word 'loudly' describes how Sanvi speaks. It modifies the verb 'speaks'.

In the sentence (b), the highlighted word 'really' modifies the adjective 'wonderful'.

In the sentence (c), the highlighted word 'too' modifies the adverb 'slowly'.

All these highlighted words are adverbs. Adverbs are words that modify a verb, adjective and another adverb. Familiarize yourself with the different types of adjectives and the examples as shown in the following figure.

Types of Adverbs	Place- describes the place of occurrence of an action. Eg. here, there, near, far, nowhere etc.,
	Time-Defines the time of occurrence of an action. Eg. tomorrow, yesterday, today, now, then, soon, immediately etc.,
	Manner-Defines how something is done. Eg. quickly, fast, well etc.,
	Degree- Defines to what degree something is done, Eg. very, quite, rather,
	Frequency- Describes how often something is done. Eg. always, never, seldom, rarely, once, occasionally.

Figure: 1   Types of Adverbs

Task 1: Frame sentences of your own using the examples of different adverbs as shown in the above diagram.

Adjectives can be changed to adverbs by adding the suffix 'ly'.

Eg. The adjective 'beautiful' becomes the adverb 'beautifully' by adding the suffix 'ly'.

Task2: Convert the following words into adverbs and use them in a sentence of your own.

polite, awkward, bitter, regular, mysterious, careful, official, anxious, generous, ferocious, bitter, accidental, natural, unfortunate, exact, legible,

Worksheet:1

1. Fill in the blanks using adverbs.

1. The meeting takes place ______________.

2. She is generally _____________ to the class.

3. The team leader ___________ discussed the new project.

4. I could not find him _______.

5. Rahim _______speaks the truth.

6. The electrician _______________ repaired the electric panel.

7. The prize money was ________ distributed among the winners.

8. One should ____________ suppress the negative thought.

9. Children shouted ___________ in the beach.

10. He _____________ placed the eggs in the basket.

11. The books are arranged __________ in the library racks.

12. I thought the movie ended _______________.

13. She __________ answered the questions asked by the police in the investigation.

14. Afrin _____________ greeted Rohit every day.

15. I am the only person in the world I should like to know ___________.

II Correct the errors from the following sentences.

1. He is enough kind to help everybody in the need.

2. If you like to succeed in life you must learn to think independent.

3. She is sure a great singer and no other singer is a match for her.

4. I came cross a friend.

5. His son's rude behaviour gives him much pain.

6. Lathika is too sick so that she cannot go to office today.

7. She is older enough to earn a living.

8. Flowers bloomed soon this spring.

9. Lakshmi sang sweet.

10. I recharge my mobile in a month.

11. Watch how careful the sparrow knits the sparrow to form a nest.

12. The students have practiced hardly for the Annual day and so, they deserve the appreciation.

13. Following the increase in tax, the Cinema halls have increased the tickets approximate ten percent.

14. She acted remarkable to achieve success.

15. Never I'll see her again.

1.4.2. Preposition

Read the following sentences, analyse carefully to find out what is wrong with them.

a) I saw your car *on* the advertisement

b) She jumped *in to* the river

c) I am afraid *with* sharks

d) We congratulate you *for* your success

e) The mountain is covered *by* snow

You might have noticed from your analysis that the meaning of the sentence changed with respect to the incorrect use of one italicized word in each sentence – *on, in to, with, for, by.* These words are prepositions which are very much essential in a sentence for conveying the proper meaning. With the incorrect use of prepositions, the expressions would become Broken English. Preposition is a word 'governing' and usually 'preceding' a noun, pronoun and expressing your relation to another word or element in the clause. Prepositions can be used to demonstrate the relationship between two words in a sentence which can be a noun, normally between a noun, verb or adjective and a noun (including proper noun) pronoun or gerund verb in the noun form as in the examples given below.

a)   Rohit ran into the classroom.

b)   The organizer sat beside the guest.

c)   I met her.

d)   Meenakshi is passionate about dancing.

1.   Forms and Functions of prepositions

There are one-word prepositions as given in the above sentences. But there are two-word prepositions which are called as complex prepositions. Prepositions that do not give literal meaning and give metaphorical meaning are called prepositional phrases. The following diagram shows the different forms of Prepositions.

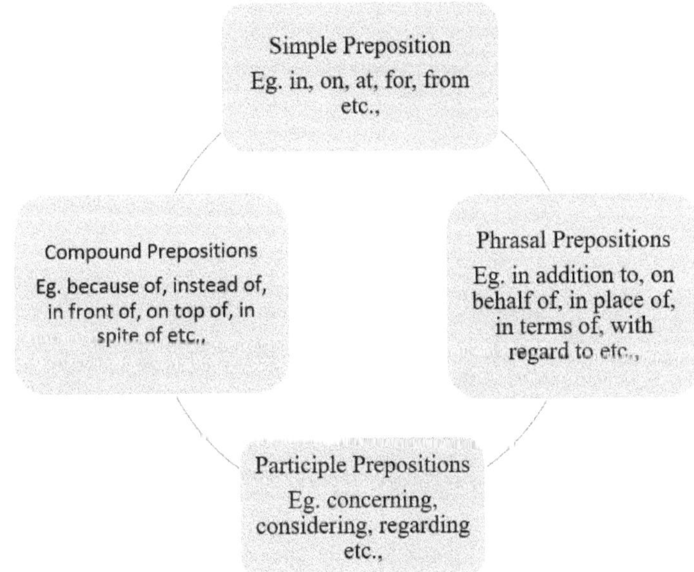

Figure 1. Forms of Prepositions

2. Functions of Prepositions

    The major functions of prepositions are that are decided upon how they relate to place, time, agent, manner and movement.

    Preposition of Place – Indicates the place or position of something or someone.

    Eg. The treasure is buried **under** the tree.

    Preposition of Time- Indicates the time factor in a sentence.

    Eg. Mahatma Gandhi was born **on** 2nd of October.

    Preposition of Agent/Manner - Describes the way anything happens or any means by which it happens.

    Eg. Children go to school **by** bus.

    Preposition of Movement- Indicates the direction in which someone or something is moving.

    Eg. He was running **towards** the stall.

3. Do you have this type of Professor in your class? Think over the highlighted words and relate to their form and functions as discussed above.

    You can sit **before** the desk or **in front of** the desk. The professor can **sit on** the desk when he's being informal or **behind** the desk and then his feet are **under** the desk or **beneath** the desk. He can stand **beside** the desk meaning **next to** the desk or **between** the desk and you. If he's clumsy, he can **bump into** the desk and stuff would **fall off** the desk. Passing his hands **over** the desk or resting his elbows **upon** the desk, he often looks **across** the desk and speaks **of** the desk or concerning the desk as if there were nothing else like the desk. Because he **thinks of** nothing except the desk, sometimes you **wonder about** the desk, what's in the **desk,** what he **paid for** the desk and if he could live without the desk. You can **walk toward** the desk, **to the desk**, **around the desk, by the desk** and even **past the desk** while he **sits at** the desk or **leans against** the desk. All of this happens of course**, in time**, during the class, **before the class, until the class, throughout the class after the class**, etc.

4. Task: Read the following mind-map on Preposition of time. Write a small story using the prepositions of Time as given in the following Mind-map.

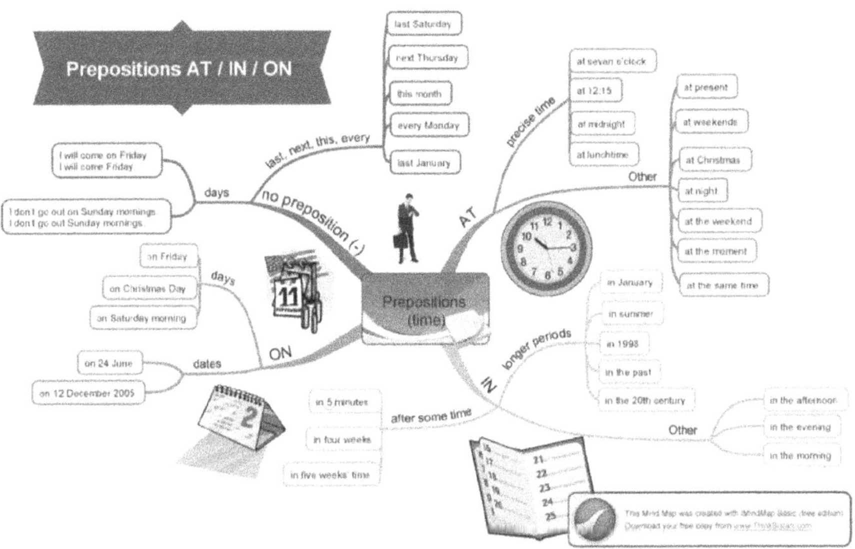

Source:https://www.researchgate.net/profile/Dian_Fadhilawati/ publication/332401470/figure/fig20/AS:747239379066881@1555167159 239/Mind-mapping-of-Preposition-of-Time.ppm retrieved on 9/12/22

Worksheet: 2

1. Fill in the blanks with suitable prepositions in the following sentences.

   i.   The history of Hindu religion dates ______ ancient time.

   ii. Nothing can deter him__________ pursuing his aim of life.

   iii. In accordance with the advice of the doctor she is ______ diet.

   iv. Cooperation between friends stems______ mutual consideration.

   v.   He is 5' 1" and he's tall ______ his age.

   vi. Strangely her name did not occur ______ me on the second meeting.

   vii. You have not to get up because the book is lying _________ hand.

   viii. In the long run, drinking proved fatal both ________ his reputation and health.

   ix. Most of the family members dissented ________ the suggestion he made.

   x.   As a dancer she has aptitude ______ classical system.

II. Correct errors in the following sentences and rewrite them.

   i.   While taking examination always write with dark ink.

   ii. The insurance company has promised to compensate the damage to my house.

   iii. You should congratulate your opponent for his grand success in the election.

   iv. My father did not agree to me on this point.

   v.   Everyone knows what for Rajasthan is famous.

   vi. Do you know he will be operated tomorrow in a Coimbatore hospital?

   vii. Ten teams are competing Singer World Cup.

   viii. I met my friend on 11 O'clock in a hotel.

ix.   She is very arrogant because she comes from a rich family

x.   A mother prays God every day for the safe return of her children.

Key for Worksheet Exercise I

i.   from/back to

ii.   from

iii.   on

iv.   from

v.   for

vi.   to

vii.   at

viii. for

ix.   from

x.   for

Key for Worksheet Exercise II

i.   'in' in the place of 'with'

ii.   'for' in the place of 'to'

iii.   'on' in the place of 'for'

iv.   'with' in the place of 'to'

v.   'for' should come after 'famous'

vi.   operated on/upon

vii.   competing 'for'

viiii.'at' in the place of 'on'

ix.   'of' in the place of 'from'

x.   prays 'to'

Unit-2
LISTENING AND SPEAKING

2.1 Introduction

This Unit focuses on the other aspects of Listening, Speaking, Reading and writing which are not dealt in the Unit 1 that has more importance to the communicative skills. It deals with the major areas such as listening to famous speeches and poems, making short speeches in formal and informal occasions, writing opinion speeches on contemporary topics, reading aloud of poems, identifying poetic devices, developing word power using idiomatic expressions, and grammar in context topics of conjunction and interjections.

The topic Listening to famous speeches highlights the significance of Listening and Speaking skills and depicts the different types of speech through a mind map. It is followed by giving strategies for delivering short speeches in formal and informal occasions with the formats of a welcome speech, Farewell Party speech and Vote of Thanks speech. Next topic deals with the Reading aloud of poems by emphasizing the Intonation and Voice Modulation. It also discusses some strategies of reading aloud along with examples and has assigned a task. This continues with describing different Figures of speech using a graphical representation. This is followed by a task for the students to identify the figures of speech from a given poem. Then Word power deals with Idioms and phrases by triggering the learners' interest to know the stories behind idioms with a story tracing the root of an idiom. This has given a set of idioms with meanings and a task for the students to frame sentences using the given idioms. The last topic Grammar in Context deals with Conjunctions and Interjections with definitions, types, examples and Grammar exercises.

2.1.1 Listening to famous speeches and poems

1. Listening to famous speeches

Listening is one of the most critical skills in life which everyone has to develop. As a child Listens to its mother in the womb, it is able to recognize the mother's voice and learns to respond to mothers' voice later and stops crying. So, the listening skill is part of everyone right before the birth. But when it comes to academics Listening is a receptive skill to trigger the productive skill speaking. It is integrated in most of the contexts and cannot be isolated. Aristotle stated the most important aspect of a public or private speech is 'to persuade'. You can see the evolution of speech from the historical speech by Mark Antony's, "Friends, **Romans, countrymen, lend me your ears!**" to the TEDx Talk of today.

Good Listening and Speaking is not just important for orators but needed for people across profession. You may be able to convince your teammates, superiors with your ideas with good speaking skill. you need to make presentations to persuade the audience for some action or give some clear picture of a scenario which others may not be aware of. Everyone needs to develop this art of listening to become a good speaker as a good listener is a good speaker. While preparing for a speech, you have to consider the occasion, purpose and the audience for the speech. For delivering various types of speech, you have to adopt different techniques and subskills. Speaking can be broadly categorized based on the purpose as given below in the mind-map:

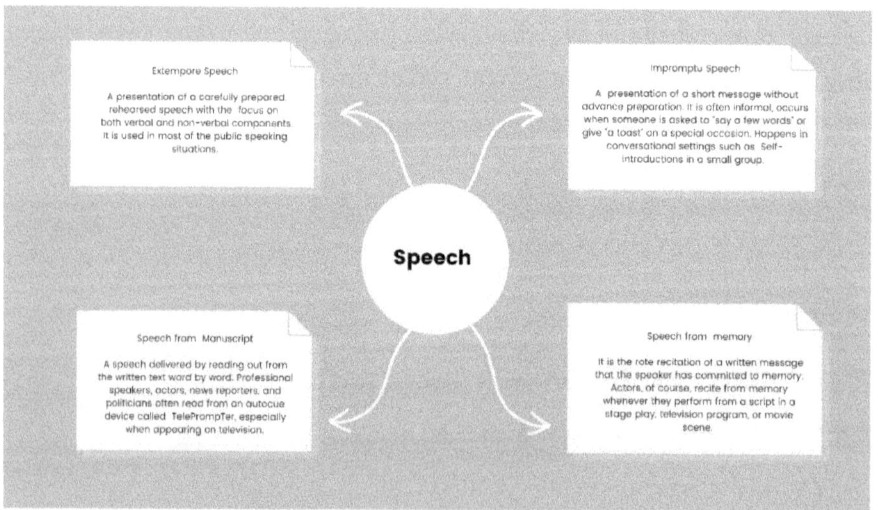

Figure: Kinds of speech

You have learnt about the importance of listening and speaking skills, different kinds of speech. But the more exposure to listening to the motivational speeches would inherently develop your speaking skills. As a lot of podcasts, TEDx talks, YouTube videos, audio and video recordings on great speakers are readily available, you can easily develop listening skills. While listening to a speech, identify the speaker, context, the main ideas, sub points, illustrations, statistics, anecdote, examples, analogies given in the speech. This enables you not only to become a good speaker but also to deliver a speech. These are the aspects to develop critical Listening skills. Listen to the speech of Dr. A. P. J. Abdul Kalam from the source link given below the transcript and critically analyse the speech

Task:

Read the transcript of the speech by Dr. APJ Abdul Kalam and analyse it as per the format given below the text.

Dr A P J Abdul Kalam: 'My vision for India', IIT Hyderabad - 2011
25 May 2011, IIT Hyderabad, Sangareddy district, Telangana, India

Source: https://speakola.com/political/dr-a-p-j-abdul-kalam-vision-for-india-2011

I have three visions for India. In 3000 years of our history people from all over the world have come and invaded us, captured our lands, conquered our minds. From Alexander onwards the Greeks, the Turks, the Moguls, the Portuguese, the British, the French, the Dutch, all of them came and looted us, took over what was ours. Yet we have not done this to any other nation. We have not conquered anyone. We have not grabbed their land, their culture and their history and tried to enforce our way of life on them. Why? Because we respect the freedom of others. That is why my FIRST VISION is that of FREEDOM. I believe that India got its first vision of this in 1857, when we started the war of Independence. It is this freedom that we must protect and nurture and build on. If we are not free, no one will respect us.

We have 10 percent growth rate in most areas. Our poverty levels are falling. Our achievements are being globally recognised today. Yet we lack the self-confidence to see ourselves as a developed nation, self-reliant and self-assured. Isn't this incorrect? MY SECOND VISION for India is DEVELOPMENT. For fifty years we have been a developing nation. It is time we see ourselves as a developed nation. We are among top five nations in the world in terms of GDP.

I have a THIRD VISION. India must stand up to the world. Because I believe that unless India stands up to the world, no one will respect us. Only strength respects strength. We must be strong not only as a military power but also as an economic power. Both must go hand-in-hand. My good fortune was to have worked with three great minds. Dr.Vikram Sarabhai, of the Dept. of Space, Professor Satish Dhawan, who succeeded him and Dr. Brahm Prakash, father of nuclear material. I was lucky to have worked with all three of them closely and consider this the great opportunity of my life.

I was in Hyderabad giving this lecture, when a 14-year-old girl asked me for my autograph. I asked her what her goal in life is. She replied: I want to live in a developed India. For her, you and I will have to build this developed India. You must proclaim India is not an underdeveloped nation; it is a highly developed nation.

You say that our government is inefficient. You say that our laws are too old. You say that the municipality does not pick up the garbage. You say that the phones don't work, the railways are a joke, the airline is the worst in the world, and mails never reach their destination. You say that our country has been fed to the dogs and is the absolute pits. You say, say and say. What do you do about it?

Dear Indians, I am echoing J.F.Kennedy's words to his fellow Americans to relate to Indians .... "ASK WHAT WE CAN DO FOR INDIA AND DO WHAT HAS TO BE DONE TO MAKE INDIA WHAT AMERICA AND OTHER WESTERN COUNTRIES ARE TODAY."

1. Write down the main ideas.

2. Write down the supporting ideas.

3. Identify the anecdotes, illustrations in the speech.

4. List out the facts and statistics supporting the main idea.

5. Note down the difficult vocabulary and find out the meaning of them from a Thesaurus

2.1.2 Making short speeches

2.1.2. a. Giving Welcome Speech in Formal occasions

You have learnt about the importance of listening to a motivational speech in the previous section. This may enable you to incorporate some speech techniques on occasions wherein you are assigned with the task of giving a speech.   In this section, we can discuss about giving a short Welcome speech / Vote of thanks on formal occasions and giving speech on informal occasions such as Farewell party and Graduation speech.

Points to remember while preparing Welcome Speech

1. Greet the audience with loud and cheerful voice.

2. Mention how special the occasion is with your captivating opening remarks.

3. Give a brief introduction about the host/organization

4. Give a brief overview of the event.

5. Welcome the speaker, key Host members, dignitaries on the dais, and audience.

6. Double check the remarks you're going to make about your guests are factually correct.

7. Conclude stating how everyone is excited to listen to the key speaker / main part of the event.

8. keep it brief. Two to three minutes is generally sufficient.

Task:

Read the following template of a Speech to Welcome the participants at a Seminar. Fill the blanks using the directions assuming a seminar taking place in your college wherein You give a welcome speech.

Very warm greetings to all the participants and the audience here for this seminar. Good morning/ Afternoon/ Evening *(choose the time of the event)*. I am feeling privileged to stand here and welcome you all to this _____________ *(name of the seminar)*. Today I, _________________ *(your name)* shall be walking you through the seminar. Before I invite the orators, I would like to introduce you to the proceeding of the event.

Firstly, I would like to thank the ___________ *(name of the hosting committee/ institute/ organisation)* for organising the _____________ *(name of the seminar)* for the benefit of the ___________ *(term for the target audience such as students, women, professionals)*. With your continuous efforts and will to do something for society and move up towards a successful and fulfilling world, we all had the opportunity to be present here, together. This informative seminar will not only guide us all but also educate us regarding a variety of this pertaining to _______________ *(purpose of the main topic of discussion in the seminar)*. On behalf of the Organisation, I would like to welcome you all and inform you that the seminar will completely enlighten you pertaining to the __________ *(the topic of the seminar)*. I kindly welcome the _________________ *(the speaker for the seminar)*, an incredible human being and a ___________ *(designation of the speaker)*. I request _________________ to introduce our Guest to this august gathering.

Thank You …

2.1.2. b. Proposing Vote of thanks in the events

The purpose of giving a Vote of thanks Speech in a program is to express the sense of gratitude. It marks the significant end of the program. It is crucial and has a dramatic impact in a way that it recognises the organizers, key speakers, and audience with a note of thanks giving and ensures the smooth conduct of the event. It is a well-authorized speech where the speaker delivers a vote of thanks to the organizer, host, and other participants. Any event can be successful only with the people who devote their resources and time to ensure that everything is flawless.

Points to remember for delivering Vote of thanks

1. Introduce yourself, role and on whose behalf giving the Vote of thanks along with the name of the event.

2. Profusely thank the Key Speakers, Organizers, Management with a note of how important their role was for the conduct of the event.

3. Highlight how the speakers motivated/inspired/entertained the audience by mentioning the main idea of the speakers.

4. Make a special mention about the Sponsors and their crucial part in the organization of the event.

5. Mention the Support staff, audience and technical team.

6. Make it brief and impressive.

You are Student Union Secretary and proposing Vote of Thanks in your college cultural program. Follow the following format prepare the speech for Vote of thanks by giving all missing details.

I, _______________ the Student Union Secretary of _______________ deem it as an honour and privilege to extend the Vote of Thanks on this occasion of _______________.

I thank _______________ for giving me the opportunity to express my gratitude on this special day.

Today we have hosted the biggest _________________ in our college.

On behalf of the ____________________I would like to thank our chief guest ______________for taking his precious time out to be the Chief Guest. Sir, indeed your words have motivated the students to take part in more cultural activities.

I thank all the Inter and Intra college students for their________________

On behalf of the _____________________, I express my heartfelt thanks to the College Management, Principal and __________________.

I would like to extend my special thanks to the Union Staff Coordinators ___________

Last but not the least, I extend my thanks to the Sponsors ___________, DJ Entertainment __________, Hospitality Partner _______________ Media Partner ______________, Digital partner ____________________without you all this cultural event would not have been possible. Thank you all very much once again.

2.1.3 Giving a speech at Informal occasions

There are some special occasions in which you may be required to give a speech like Farewell party, Graduation speech and Toast Speech. The formalities of such speech are different from formal speech.

1. Preparing for an informal speech

    1. Instead of reading out from a script or notes, start with a casual greeting and engage the audience in a conversational and heartfelt way.

    2. Speak audibly and loudly in case there is no microphone arrangements so as to ensure everyone hears and understands the speech.

3. Stay calm and speak in a relaxed tone and engage the audience in a casual manner. You can be a little emotional also while saying 'Goodbye'.

4. Use humour as smiling and laughing with the audience promotes more engagement.

5. Use natural gestures to make your speech genuine and honest.

6. Highlight all positive things about the people /organization and express your sense of gratitude on how you had a good time working with the organization.

Sample of a Short Farewell Speech

Good morning to everyone presents here to witness the farewell of the batch 2020- 2023. It's my honour to give a short farewell speech about my student life. It's with a heavy heart that I begin my speech today and I can believe that my classmates would understand how much we are going to miss this beautiful campus once we are graduated from here.

I can undoubtedly say that we are going to miss this place and as the saying goes the magic is not in the place but the people that surround it. I don't have any regrets in my life and I am grateful for the last three years at this campus. I met beautiful people that included my friends, my professors, and all the non-teaching staff. They all played an important role in my life and helped in shaping me into the man I am today.

Everyone here is friendly, especially the faculty members who helped us whenever we had doubts in any subject. On behalf of everyone, I can proudly say that you made us into better people and helped us face all the challenges that life would throw at us in the future.

Thank you for helping us. I would like to conclude my short farewell speech by saying that I have a small message for my friends that this farewell is not the end, it cannot be the end of the memories and bonds we created with each other throughout all these years.

I can surely say that life would not be easy from now on and there will be a lot of challenges that would be thrown at us in the future. But let us promise not to forget each other. Let we will be there whenever someone needs help in the future.

Let us promise that we will be in touch with each other. Remember that this farewell is a goodbye to our college days and can never be for our friendship, thank you.

(Source:https://www.vedantu.com/english/farewell-speech-for-students)

Sample for Graduation Speech;

Welcome friends, family, and teachers that helped me get to where I am today. It is an honor to be standing before you on such a memorable occasion.

I want to start out by saying thank you to all my friends, family, and most of all, my Savior who is Jesus Christ for helping me every step of the way.

It has been an amazing journey and one my fellow Class of 2014 members will most likely never forget.

Four years ago, the Class of 2014 was just walking through the doors of Landrum High School and we have had many memories over the course of our high school journey. We all had one goal in mind and that was to make our mark on the school that we attended and make our mark on the world once we graduate. We all have different career choices but we're all bound by the same common cause and that is to GRADUATE!

We are your Class of 2014 not just because we scooted our way past every year but because we put in the hard work and the effort to get to where we are today and we could not have done that without the friends, family and teachers constantly encouraging us to keep up the good work.

It's not all about if you look good, or fit in at your school, it's about the legacy that you will leave once you graduate.

Dr. Seuss once said, "You're off to great places, TODAY is your DAY, Your mountain is waiting, so get on your way!"

I pray that the Class of 2014 will walk out of here today feeling proud of all they have accomplished over these last four years. And always remember, it's not about the friends that you make while you're in school, it's the memories that you leave behind that really count.

Source:https://www.best-speech-topics.com/sample-high-school-graduation-speech.html

Task

1. Your Organization/Company is bidding you Farewell after your retirement. Write a Short Farewell Speech that you will be delivering on the occasion.

2. You are completing PG Degree and your department Juniors are giving a Farewell party to your batch. Prepare a Short Farewell Party Speech that you will be delivering on the occasion.

2.2 Reading and Writing

2.2.1 Writing Opinion piece on contemporary topics

You are taught Proverbial Paragraph writing in the previous unit. This unit deals with writing opinion essays on contemporary topics such as food, lifestyle and travel. Also, it can be film or book review writing. In this world of social media exchange of ideas, sharing of opinion on travel, food, film, book in the form of review or on any contemporary topic is having relevance and significance. It is not that we are always the passive consumers of others opinion but we can differ and express opposite and contrary opinion also. This reflects one's critical thinking skills. Op-eds and Blog writing are the important medium to share one's views either by agreeing or contradicting or stating different opinion on any contemporary issue. You may be familiar with diary writing which is a record of happening of day-today events. You might be taught Journal writing also. Let us discuss about Op-ed writing.

1. What does Op-eds stand for?

    Op-eds are one of the most powerful tools in communications today. Op-eds became a way for people to simply express their opinions in the media. They are written by experts, observers, or someone who is passionate about a topic. As media in general does not scrutinize or support anyone or group to share their opinion, op-eds have become more and more common these days. You all know an Editorial Column published in the newspaper. This is written by a member of a publication's board or editors, and they are meant to represent the view of the publication. The main purpose of this is to inform the public about something. Apart from this it has the other purpose of persuading the readers on a controversial issue. Op-eds, on the other hand, are "opposite the editorial" page columns. They began as a way for an author to present an opinion that opposed the one on the editorial board. An op-ed is different from Letter to the editor, which is when someone writes a note to complain about an article, and that note is published.

Task: Read the Op.ed article from the link below and familiarize yourself about the style of writing.

https://www.agoda.com/press/op-ed-the-future-of-travel?cid=1844104

https://timesofindia.indiatimes.com/blogs/voices/metaverse-a-new-brand-playground/

2. Format and Strategies for writing opinion piece

    - Introduce the thread of argument and capture the readers' attention with example, illustration, anecdote and startling statistics.

    - Logically build your argument by sticking to your argument of either supporting or opposing the point of discussion.

- Without beating about the bush, avoiding jargons, use simple language by paying more attention to clarity of thought and expression.

- Be consistent throughout your argument and don't mess up by switching over your stand in between.

- Be precise and specific in your expression. Avoid high sounding words and vocabulary. Always use simple sentences and active voice.

- Offer solutions by clarifying your stand with supporting details for the advantages and disadvantages over the topic of discussion.

- Length of an opinion essay can be of 500-750 words. It can have short paragraphs based upon the development of argument.

- Give a winning conclusion with strong emphasis upon the points of highlights of your argument.

3. Sample Opinion piece Essay on Fast food

Read this opinion essay and analyse how the above strategies are adopted in writing this.

Many people think that fast food has affected our health and family relationships. What is your opinion?

McDonalds, Burger King, Pizza Hut and Hardees are just some of the many fast-food outlets that can now be seen across most cities in the world. With our demanding work schedules eating into leisure time, it is no wonder that many people take advantage of the quick take away fast food. Many people believe that fast food affects our health and family relationships and I agree with this. I believe it has a negative effect on both these issues.

First of all, fast food has been proven to be one of the causes that can lead to heart disease and obesity. Look at the many fast-food menus and you will always see hamburgers, other meat and chicken cooked in oil and of course French fries. All these foods are cooked in oil which is full of harmful fats. It is these fats that cause problems with our arteries which may lead to heart disease. In addition, people nowadays are working longer hours and exercising less. They do not have enough time to go home and cook a meal after a long day at work. It is much easier to drive into a fast-food restaurant, order and pay and then drive away. At many places you do not even have to get out of your car. Eating fast food and reducing exercise can only lead to health problems.

Secondly, fast food also affects family relationships. In the past families were a strong unit. This strong relationship was helped by the family sitting together and eating together. Problems were discussed and solutions found while eating dinner. Nowadays with streets full of fast-food places and advertising on every corner and every channel on TV, young people, especially young men, prefer meeting their friends and going to fast-food restaurants. Staying at home and eating with the family is not considered 'cool'. As a consequence, parents are seeing less and less of their children and there is no 'quality time' where parents and children are able to sit down and discuss things. The family relationship begins to break down.

In conclusion, while fast food will never disappear, it is the responsibility of the parents to guide and educate their children in regard to good eating habits. Also asking children to be home for meals so families may eat and talk together will keep the family relationships strong.

Source: https://www.5staressays.com/blog/opinion-essay/opinion-essay-about-fast-food.pdf

4. Writing book / film review

    Opinion writing has other forms such as book or film review writing. This enables the students to analyse the story, theme, characters and the author or director's ideas. Book /Film review writing is a good practice to develop critical thinking and writing skills. It also helps students to learn how to critically evaluate a book / film and support given ideas with facts and examples. This reflects one's analytical, critical and reflective skills.

5. Format for writing a book review

    Here are some important guidelines that you can follow on how to format a book review.

1. Begin with the basic bibliographical information of the book such as its title, author's name and publisher's details.

2. The classification/ type /series of the book and should be included in the opening clause.

3. Write about the main theme in the following section and include a few sentences to summarize the text.

4. The next step is to introduce the main characters of the book to your readers. Provide an objective description of the important parts of the story.

5. Provide a vivid description of the main setting and interesting information about the story to keep your readers engaged.

6. Clarify the purpose of the story and summarize the plot by answering the following questions.

    What are the goals of each character in the story?

    What is the main conflict in the plot?

    Were the conflicts resolved?

7. Finally, write about the main message that the author has tried to convey to his readers.

8. Provide a final assessment of the book and support it with specific examples.

6. Sample book Review

    Go through the given below book review and analyse the key components of it.

I Capture the Castle

Review by Lauren W., age 17, Mensa in Georgia

Dodie Smith's novel I Capture the Castle is a journey through the mind of a young writer as she attempts to chronicle her daily life. Seventeen-year-old Cassandra Mortmain has recently learned to speed-write, and she decides to work on her writing skills by describing the actions and conversations of those around her.

Cassandra lives in a fourteenth-century English castle with an interesting cast of characters: her beautiful older sister, Rose; her rather unsociable author father and his second wife, artist-model Topaz; Stephen, the garden boy; a cat and a bull terrier; and sometimes her brother Thomas when he is home from school. One fateful day they make the acquaintance of the Cotton family, including the two sons, and a web of tangled relationships ensues.

While I definitely recommend this book to other readers, I would recommend it to older teenagers, mainly because it will resonate better with them. The writing is tame enough that younger teens could also read it, but most of the characters are adults or on the verge of adulthood. Older readers would take the most from it since they can not only relate, but they may also better pick up on and appreciate Cassandra's sometimes subtle humour.

Over the course of the novel, Cassandra undergoes a definite transformation from child to mature young adult, even though it's only over the course of several months. I love that I could see into her mindset and read exactly what she was feeling when she thought out situations. Her thoughts flowed well and moved the book along very quickly.

Cassandra's narrative voice is wonderful. She is serious at times, but also very witty, which makes for an engaging read. It feels absolutely real, as though I'm reading someone's actual journal. Sometimes I forget that I am reading a story and not a real-life account. Her emotions and the dialogue are so genuine, and they are spot-on for a seventeen-year-old girl in her situation.

Cassandra has many wonderful insights on life, on topics ranging from writing to faith to matters of the heart. I personally have had some of the same thoughts as Cassandra, except Ms. Smith was able to put them into words.

Capture the Castle should be essential reading for aspiring writers, those looking for historical fiction or romance, or anyone who loves reading amazing classic books. Dodie Smith is an exceptional writer, and I Capture the Castle is a book that will never become obsolete.

Source:https://www.studocu.com/ph/document/university-of-san-carlos/english/i-capture-the-castle-grade-12/18460899

7. Writing film review

Having familiarized with writing an opinion essay, book review writing, we can move to film review writing. This can be customized in lines of book review writing. You have to assess some additional details such as dialogue, camera techniques, use of colours, costumes, light, music symbol and audience's reaction in the theatre. You can read below given film review on Avatar -2 published in the Times of India.

Avatar: The Way Of Water Movie Review : A worthy sequel that's dazzlingly immersive and hypnotic

Story: A worthy sequel to the 2009 film Avatar, James Cameron takes us back to the stunning world of Pandora, where human turned Na'vi Jake Sully (Sam Worthington) and Na'vi princess Ney'tiri (Zoe Saldaña) must do everything it takes to protect their children from the 'sky people' (humans from earth).

Review: "The way of water connects all things. The sea is our home before our birth and after we die." Beyond the 3D visual spectacle that Avatar is, something we trust James Cameron to deliver, the franchise's beauty lies in its underlying spiritual arc and ode to continuity of life. Life finds a way. It evolves no matter the surroundings as love is transformative.

Humans call the Na'vi 'hostiles and insurgents', when it is they who forcefully infiltrate and occupy their land. Despite its magical, fictional setting, Avatar is not devoid of socio-political themes. It addresses race, civilisation, takes a strong anti-military stand and makes a plea for environment conservation through its simple story of parents and children. A spectacular climax revolves around parents protecting their children and vice versa.

From lush jungles to the gorgeous reefs... the action shifts from forests to the sea this time around and it's equally meditative and hypnotic. For over three hours you find yourself immersed in the enchanting world of an oceanic clan (Metkayina) or the reef people who give Sully and his family a refuge from humans. The sequel scores high on action and emotion. One is not compromised for the other. 'Happiness is simple. The Sullys stay together. This is our biggest weakness and our greatest strength," says Jake Sully and the story embodies that spirit. The tale isn't unique per se but the storytelling and visual excellence are otherworldly epic. Mounted on a massive scale, not once do you find yourself wanting to return to the real world.

> **While the predecessor set the bar high for visual effects 13 years ago, the new film takes it a step further. Like the previous film, the director does not use 3D as a gimmick but uses it artfully to accentuate audience immersion in the world and story. Avatar: The Way of Water deserves be watched in IMAX 3D. It is the greatest immersive cinema experience of the year — world building at its finest.**
>
> Source : TIMES OF INDIA https://timesofindia.indiatimes.com/ entertainment/english/movie-reviews/avatar-the-way-of-water/movie-review/96219578.cms

2.3. Reading poetry

2.3.1 Reading aloud of a poem with Intonation and Voice Modulation

1. Reading aloud of a poem

    Poems were created to be heard. poems are aural compositions which means they are meant for listening. Poets compose their works with the ear in mind. A good poetry works better through the ears than through the eyes. As poetry is composed for singing, it has proper metre and rhythm and stress pattern. One should learn the importance of these and put special attention to bring out these nuances, the reading aloud of the poem may bring out the beauty of the composition. Poetry evokes some emotions among the readers. Reading aloud a poetry is different from reading aloud a prose. Reading out a poem with intonation and voice modulation is quite important.

    Let us discuss about stress, rhythm, intonation and voice modulation in detail with example.

    Stress is where the sound is stressed in a syllable. For example, the stress is on the second syllable in the word *'baNAna'* whereas in the word *'ORange'* the stress is on the first syllable.

Rhythm is about how we use a combination of stressed and unstressed words in sentences. Sentences have strong beats (the stressed words) and weak beats (the unstressed words). A poem is iambic if you start with an unstressed syllable, and then alternate stressed and unstressed. So, you can find the alternating stress in this Shakespeare's famous line "It is the star to every wandering bark." as given below:

it IS the STAR to EV-ery WAN-der-ING bark.

Intonation is the way the pitch of a speaker's voice goes up or down as they speak. We use intonation to help get our message across. Intonation is the changing of tone in a person's voice when sounding out particular words. It often reflects emotion and makes emphasis upon the attitudes when speaking. To demonstrate intonation, arrows are used to represent each fall or rise [↘][↗]. And in poetry the symbols (/) (\) are used to mark Rising and Falling -Intonation respectively. There are three different types of intonations such as Rising -Intonation, Falling-Intonation and Fall-rise Intonation are used in poetry to emphasize upon the theme in terms of stress pattern and rhyming scheme.

- Rising -tone (/) is used to express various emotions, such as non-finality, incompleteness, question, surprise, doubt, hesitation, interest, request and suggestion, politeness and rhetoric questions.

- Falling -intonation (\) is used in statements, declarative sentences, special questions, commands and exclamatory sentences.

- Fall-Rise Intonation (\ /) is the way that the voice both falls then rises in between the words. This is used to denote uncertainty, confusion and special emphasis.

Task

Listen to this Robert Frost's Poem to relate your understanding about these tonal variations and also apply it to the transcript of the poem indicated with these tonal symbols.

(Source: https://usefulenglish.ru/phonetics/listening-for-intonation-fire-and-ice)

Text of Audio 1 (AmE), with intonation marked

'Fire and \ICE by 'Robert \FROST

('Read for 'librivox 'dot /org by E'lizabeth Mc\Andrew.)

'Some 'say the 'world will 'end in \FIRE, | |

'Some 'say in \ICE. | |

From what 'I've 'tasted of de'sire |

I 'hold with 'those who 'favor \FIRE. | |

'But | if it had to 'perish 'TWICE |

I 'think I 'know e'nough of 'HATE |

To 'know that for de'struction 'ICE

Is \ALso 'great |

And would suf\FICE. | |

('End of \poem. 'This re'cording is in the 'public do\main.)

2. Strategies for Reading aloud a poem in the classroom

1. Remember poetic lines as the measure of music and read with the flow of rhythm without jarring separations.

2. Think of the end of a line as signalling a slight pause, even if the line ends without punctuation and give appropriate slight pauses wherever necessary.

3. Unlike reading a report, poetry is communicating the emotions. Pay attention to emphasize the poetic devices such as repetition, tonal variations, alliteration and rhyme.

4. Slow down and let the poetic language come alive. Adjust the volume high or low, pause between words and make the lines really resonate with you.

5. Keep good public speaking practices in mind, such as confident posture and eye contact with the audience.

Task 1

Tune in your ears to these podcasts and practice reading aloud of poetry.

https://www.poetryfoundation.org/podcasts

3. Rhyming Scheme of Poetry

    Let us analyse the rhyming scheme of the poem 'A Dirge' by Christina Rossetti which is given below. The poem has two stanzas. In the first stanza, the opening two lines rhyme together with the ending words *'falling'* and *'calling'* which is denoted by AA. In the third and fourth lines the words *'cluster'* and *'muster'* rhyme together but different from the previous set. Hence it is denoted as BB. The fifth- and sixth-line rhyme together with the words *'flying'* and *'dying'* and denoted by CC. This is repeated in the second stanza also. Hence this poem has the rhyming scheme of AABBCC.

A Dirge

By <u>Christina Rossetti</u>

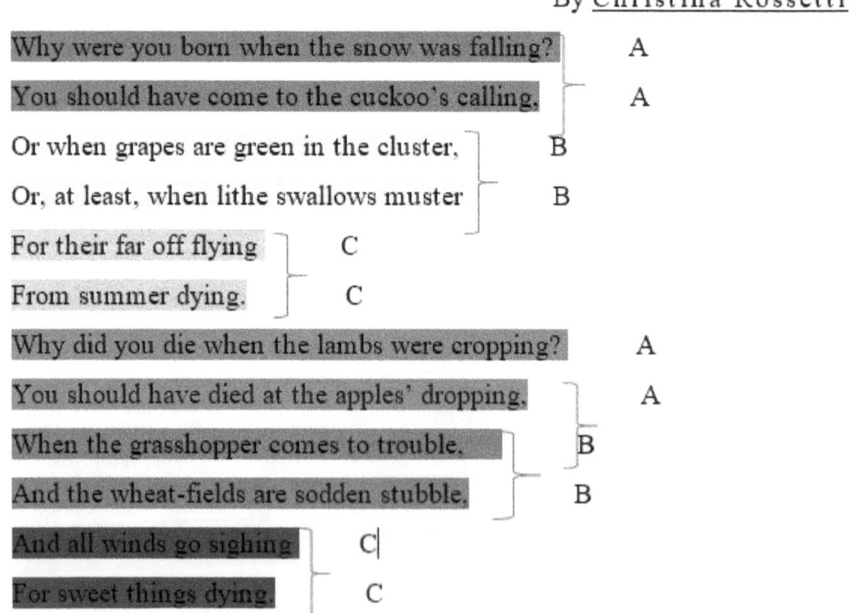

4. Identifying and using figures of speech in a poem

Language of a poem is different from the language of a prose. How a crown is embedded with stones and diamonds to add more beauty, a poem is embellished with all poetic devices. Knowing the definition of the poetic devices enables the readers to understand and appreciate the poem. The common poetic devices such as Simile, Metaphor, Personification, Assonance, Alliteration and Rhetorical questions are discussed in the below figure with examples. Read this and enrich your knowledge and understanding about poetic devices.

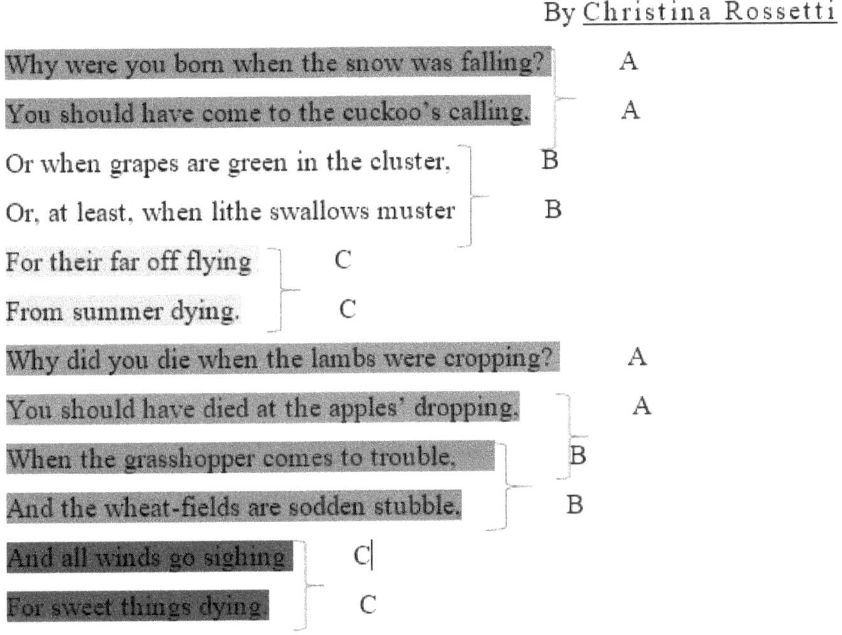

Fig. Poetic Devices

Let us apply the definitions of the above poetic devices in this poem given below which are pointing out.

All the world's a stage

– William Shakespeare

All the world's a stage, ⟶ Metaphor
And all the men and women merely players;
They have their exits and their entrances;
And one man in his time plays many parts,
His acts being seven ages. At first the infant,
Mewling and puking in the nurse's arms;
And then the whining school-boy, with his satchel
And shining morning face, creeping like snail ⟶ Simile
Unwillingly to school. And then the lover, Personification/ Simile
Sighing like furnace, with a woeful ballad
Made to his mistress' eyebrow. Then a soldier,
Full of strange oaths, and bearded like the pard, ⟶ Simile
Jealous in honour, sudden and quick in quarrel,
Seeking the bubble reputation   Personification
Even in the cannon's mouth. And then the justice, ⟶ Metaphor
In fair round belly with good capon lin'd,
With eyes severe and beard of formal cut,
Full of wise saws and modern instances;
And so he plays his part. The sixth age shifts
Into the lean and slipper'd pantaloon,
With spectacles on nose and pouch on side;
His youthful hose, well sav'd, a world too wide ⟶ Alliteration
For his shrunk shank; and his big manly voice,
Turning again toward childish treble, pipes
And whistles in his sound. Last scene of all,
That ends this strange eventful history,
Is second childishness and mere oblivion;
Sans teeth, sans eyes, sans taste, sans everything.
Task 2 Read the below given poem and answer the questions that follow.

My Shadow

– Robert Louis Stevenson

I have a little shadow that goes in and out with me,
And what can be the use of him is more than I can see.
He is very, very like me from the heels up to the head;
And I see him jump before me, when I jump into my bed.
The funniest thing about him is the way he likes to grow—
Not at all like proper children, which is always very slow;
For he sometimes shoots up taller like an India-rubber ball,
And he sometimes gets so little that there's none of him at all.

He hasn't got a notion of how children ought to play,
And can only make a fool of me in every sort of way.
He stays so close beside me, he's a coward you can see;
I'd think shame to stick to nursie as that shadow sticks to me!

One morning, very early, before the sun was up,
I rose and found the shining dew on every buttercup;
But my lazy little shadow, like an arrant sleepy-head,
Had stayed at home behind me and was fast asleep in bed.

Answer the following questions.

i.   Write two pairs of rhyming words from the poem.

ii. 'an arrogant sleepy-head' refers to __________

iii. What figures of speech is used in the following? Explain briefly.

iv. For he sometimes shoots up taller like an India-rubber ball

v.   Why do you think the shadow is a coward?

vi. When and why did the shadow part the author?

vii. What are the funniest ways of the growth of the shadow boy?

viii. Identify the poetic devices from the poem and give examples from the poetic lines.

ix. Identify alliterations and consonants in the poetry, if there are any.

2.4 Word Power

2.4.1 Idioms and Phrases

1.   Knowing the stories behind idioms

Idiomatic expressions in English language always leave the non-native speakers of English to play peek-a-boo with meaning and usage. The given dialogue between a native and non-native speaker posits the difficulty of using idiomatic expressions in real life conversation.

Native speaker: "I feel a bit under the weather today."

Non-native speaker: Yes, weather is very bad today.

Native speaker: (Looks confused).

The meaning of the idiomatic expression 'under the weather' is unwell / sick / ill. The non-native speaker related it to the bad weather of the day.

Read and infer the meaning of the idiom given in the below sentence.

It is raining *cats and dogs* today.

If you literally translate the words cat and dogs to get the meaning of the idiom and you can get this below picture in the mind. Do you think is it possible to get this type of rain?

These problems related to the misunderstanding that arise out of the use of idioms by non-native speakers. This is due to the non-native speaker's way of understanding the meaning of the idiom by literal translation of each word. But idiomatic expressions don't give literal meanings but metaphorical meaning. As idioms are surrounded by some etymological tales, it is easy for the learners to associate their meaning once they know the story behind the idiomatic expressions. The following story behind the idiom 'seize the opportunity with its forelock' make the learners understand the meaning of the idiom and enable them to use in the context.

> *Every onlooker was puzzled at a painting in an art exhibition for the figure was quirky. A human face was painted in such a way that his hair was grown from the forehead covering the entire face and the head was bald. The artist who was around there was approached for any significance or interpretation of the painting. The artist replied pointing at the figure 'this is the man called 'opportunity' who invariably passes by everyone and unnoticed by many as he is beyond noticeable in the hustle-bustles of routine busy life. As his face is masked by hair, it is hard for anyone to recognise him in a glance. Only after the man had passed by, many people could figure out the man as 'opportunity' and rush up to catch him only to end up in vain for his bald head yields them nothing to grab and pull. This is how the opportunity-man gives butter hands to many. But a few has the intuitive power to identify at the spur of the moment, facing him in front and capture it with its forelock. They are the ones who **'seize the opportunity with its forelock'***

2. How idioms are different from phrasal verbs and proverbs?

    Read and analyse the following sentences. Identify and mark the italicized words as idiomatic expressions and phrasal verbs.

    a) You are going to act in the drama today. It is sure, you will *break a leg*!

    b) The war *broke out* in 1914.

    c) At times of difficulties, one has *to get along with things*.

    d) I suppose I could *get on* with reading while waiting.

    e) The Manager promised him that he will *look into* the issue.

In the sentence a) *break a leg* is an idiom giving the meaning of wishing good luck.

In the sentence b) *broke out* is a phrasal verb that is the verb break used with the preposition out giving the meaning of something dangerous breaks out.

In the sentence c) *to get along with* is an idiom giving the meaning of to calm down.

In the sentence d) *get on* is a phrasal verb that is the verb *get* used with the preposition *on* giving the meaning of starting something.

In the sentence e) *look into is* a phrasal verb that is the verb *look is* used with the preposition into giving the meaning of investigate something.

It is clear from the above examples that idiomatic expressions give metaphorical meanings and are fixed expressions whereas phrasal verbs are verbs used with prepositions and adverbs.

Idiomatic expressions are different from proverbs. Proverbs are a saying or a short sentence to give an advice or teach moral.

3.   Frame sentences of your own using the idioms given below.

Idioms	Meaning	Sentences
kick the bucket	to die	Eg.Gopal kicked the bucket as he incurred huge loss in the business.
ball is in your court	It is up to you to take the next decision.	
cup of tea	one's Favourite activity	
Beat about the bush	not coming to a point of discussion	
Once in a blue moon	An act that happens rarely	
Pull someone's leg	To make fun of someone	
To cast an arm and leg	Something very expensive	

Idioms	Meaning	Sentences
A piece of cake	Something very easy to perform	
Think outside the box	To think creatively	
Straight from the horse's mouth	To get the information directly from the person who is the source of the information	

Worksheet 1

Fill in the blanks by choosing the correct idiom from the box given below.

> finding my feet, go down in flames, piece of cake, sticky fingers, in the red, hit the sack, cut corners, make ends meet

a) I thought the interview would be difficult but it was a piece of cake.

b) Children needs to ______________ early to get up on time.

c) 'How are you doing in Singapore?' 'I'm still______________.'

d) The supervisor was fired because he had ______________.

e) Sometimes cab drivers try to ____________ to avoid the traffic.

f) 'If you will not plan properly your dreams can ____________.

g) I don't earn much from my job as a freelance writer, but I can____________.

h) 'Do you think you could lend me some money?' 'No, I am __________ this month'.

2.5 Conjunctions

Conjunctions play an important role in the unity of sentences. An orderly arrangement of facts, ideas merging with the other facts or ideas and logical progression of thoughts help to achieve unity in text. The sequence of elements in logical order is important for organising a sentence. To achieve the purpose of bringing unity in a sentence, construct a sentence with paying attention for Conjunction as they are connecting the various elements and convey appropriate meaning. Let us consider the following;

The lesson is interesting and informative, but it is very much lengthy. And also, the vocabulary is very difficult.

The first sentence of these two sentences mentions two positive points and one negative point. The second sentence is a negative sentence. To achieve sentence unity and logicality, you can bring all positive points in one sentence and the negative points in the other as given below.

Revised: The lesson is interesting and informative. But it is very much lengthy and has difficult vocabulary.

In this coherent sentence, the reader has no difficulty in moving from part to part and understand the writer's thought.

With this example, you have learnt how significant the role of conjunction in the unity of a sentence. Conjunctions can be defined as a part of speech that is used to connect words, phrases, clauses, or sentences. They can be one word or a few words. They glue words, phrases and clauses together and are made to convey two ideas in one sentence. They can be broadly divided into two as Co-ordinating and Sub-ordinating conjunctions based on their functions. Co-ordination and Sub-ordination are the devices by which the writer gives different degrees of emphasis to the different parts of his sentence. Co-ordinating Conjunctions join the two of the below given sentence elements which have the same grammatical value:

Words to words

Phrases to phrases

Clause to clauses

Sentences to sentences

Examples for Co-ordinating conjunctions are For, and, nor, but, or, yet, so. Remember the mnemonic FANBOYS to relate to these coordinating conjunctions.

Eg. 'For' – is used to explain the 'why'. She will be late for the meeting for she has an appointment with the doctor.

'And' – is used when two similar clauses or points are made. Rohit and Pradeep live on my street.

'Nor' – is used about similar two items but in a negative sense. She is neither aggressive nor talkative.

'But' – is generally used to show a contrast between two clauses. I like living in Hillside region but my friend likes living in a coastal area.

'Or' – is used to suggest an alternative. Do your assignment or you will be losing internal marks.

'Yet' – is used to show a contrast in spite of something. Sanya knew it was naughty, yet she did it anyway.

'So' – is used to show a result of something. I've just bought the Instant Cake Mix that my daughter wanted, so she will be baking cake.

You have learnt from these examples Co-ordinating conjunctions join two sentence elements with the same grammatical value whereas subordinating conjunctions join sentence elements with different grammatical value. In other words, they join: words to phrases, phrases to clauses, clause to sentences, etc.

Another way to think of subordinating conjunctions is as a link between two clauses of a complex sentence where one of the clauses is an independent clause and the other is a subordinate clause.

There are many subordinating conjunctions but the most common are: after, although, as, as if, because, before, how, if, since, than, though, unless, until, when, where and while.

Let us discuss how coordinating and subordinating conjunctions are used to join sentences and within the sentences.

Co-ordinate Conjunctions to join Statements	Co-ordinate Conjunctions to join Contrasting Statements	Co-ordinate Conjunctions to join Alternate Statements	Co-ordinate Conjunctions to join Inference with Another Statement
And not only .... but also... as well as both...and...	But Yet Whereas Nevertheless While though...yet	Or Either..or Nor Neither...nor Otherwise Else Still neither	For so

Sub-ordinating Conjunctions	Introduces Adverb Clauses
Since, before, after, as, when, whenever, till, one's, now, that, as soon as, while	Adverb clause of time
Where, wherever, everywhere	Adverb clause of place
As, as if, as though, in that, if	Adverb clause of manner
Because, since, in as much as, that, in so far as	Adverb clause of cause
That, in order that, so that, and lest	Adverb clause of purpose
So that, so.... that, such.... that	Adverb clause of result or consequence
If, unless, whether, that, provided, and so long as	Adverb clause of condition
Though, although, even if, even though, while, whereas	Adverb clause of concession
How much, how little, how many? As, as.....as, so....as, than	Adverb clause of Degree or Comparison

Familiarize yourselves by going through the following sentences formed using Co-ordinating and Sub-ordinating Conjunctions.

1. Jaipur is a tourist city and it is famous for forts and palaces.

2. Vedha is not only honest but also intelligent.

3. The ski champion enjoys winter sports as well as cooking.

4. He may either invest his money in a business or spend for his family.

5. Neither Tom nor his parents answered the phone call.

6. All my brothers are Chartered Accountants whereas I am a Writer.

7. Invest your money wisely, else /otherwise you will lose the hard-earned money.

8. I drink coffee whenever I have headache.

9. Although Rahim is poor, he is always helping others.

10. As soon as the driver applied sudden break, many in the bus fell down.

Worksheet Exercise

1. Combine the sentences using the conjunctions given in brackets:

You will catch the bus. Run fast. (if)

I will meet you. I finish my work. (when)

She will buy a saree. She will buy a Salwar set. (either...or)

He is intelligent. He is hard working. (neither ..... nor).

Radha is a good vocalist. she is also a good dancer. (not only .... but also)

He waited. The rain stopped. (till)

You will lose money. You invest wisely. (unless)

It was raining. I couldn't leave my home. (so much.... that)

He sold the house. He was in need of money. (because)

She struggles hard. She finds it difficult to make ends meet. (Yet)

2. Fill in the blanks by choosing the appropriate Co-ordinating Conjunction given below.

however, But, or, nor, whereas, and, so, yet,

1.   Would you rather have nuts _____gems on your ice cream as topping?

2.   His two favourite sports are cricket _______ tennis.

3.   I wanted to go to the temple, ________ my friend refused.

4.   I am allergic to cats, _______ I have two of them.

5.   I am a strict vegetarian, ________ I don't eat any meat.

6.   Rita does not like to swim, _____ does she enjoy cycling.

7.   Mithika is rich __________ her sister is poor

8.   He tried to solve the problem, ________ difficult it is.

2.6 Interjection

2.6.1 What is interjection?

Interjection is the last among the eight parts of speech. It demonstrates the sudden burst of feelings or emotions. It is defined as a word or phrase that is grammatically independent from the words around it, and mainly expresses feeling rather than meaning (https://www.merriam-webster. com/dictionary/interjection). It can be placed before or after a sentence. Usually, *interjections* are followed by an exclamation point. They are common in speech and are much more common in electronic messages than in other types of writing.

Examples:

Oh, what a beautiful house!
Uh-oh! this looks bad.
Well! it's time to say good night.
I can't believe I lost the key! *Ugh*!

The table below gives a list of interjections which express varied sentiments such as surprise, disgust, joy, fear, relief, etc.

S. No.	Interjection	Feeling	Example
1.	Hi! Hello! Hey! Happy birthday!	greeting	Hello! How are you?
2.	Bye! Good-bye! See ya!	bidding farewell	Bye! See you.
3.	Hurrah! Hooray! Wow! Yay! Yeah!	joy	Hurrah! I have passed the exam! Hooray! Our team won. Wow! I'm so happy for you. Yay! We did it. Yeah! I love orange juice.
4.	Hmm! Um! Er! Uh!	doubt	Hmm! I'm not sure about that..
5.	What! Ah! Oh! Wow! Eek! Well! My goodness! Oh my God!	Surprise / amazement	What! I can't believe it. Oh! What a nice view. Ah! My mom is at home. Eek! It moved at last. Well! So she got a job. My goodness! How did you miss it? Oh my God! Save me.
6.	Bravo! Good!	approval	Bravo! You have done a good job. Good! Now we move on to the next chapter.

S. No.	Interjection	Feeling	Example
7.	Help! Eek! Oops!	fear / panic / dismay	Help! I'm going to fall. Oops! I almost spilled my coffee.
8.	Yuck! Er! Ugh! Eww!	disgust	Yuck! This peanut butter is disgusting. Er! This apple is rotten. Ugh! I can't stand his idiocy. Eww! The movie was so gory.
9.	Alas!	pity	Alas! My funds have some limitations.
10.	Ouch! Ah! Oh! Alas!	grief / pain	Ouch! That hurts me. Ah! I hurt my toe. Alas! The city has been captured.
11.	Shh! Hush!	desire for silence	Shh! The show is about to start.
12.	Uh oh!	dismay	Uh oh! The teacher has caught him while using bits.
13.	Phew! Whew!	relief	I didn't do my homework. But the teacher didn't check. Phew! Whew! I can't believe we actually finished.
14.	Great! Well done! Brilliant! Bravo! Wow! Congrats!	admiration / praise/ appreciation	Well done! You did great. Wow! That's really great news. Congrats! Finally you got your Master's degree.
15.	Yay! Yippee!	Celebration	Yay! The exams are over. Yippee! We won. Let's walk to the mall.

S. No.	Interjection	Feeling	Example
16.	Ho-hum!	boredom	Look at all this paper work. Ho-hum!
17.	Hmph! Argh!	frustration / anger/ irritation	Don't call me. It's your mistake. Hmph! Argh! The bike doesn't start.
18.	Yippee!	accomplishment	Yippee! I bought a new house.
19.	Look! Listen! Shh!	To draw attention	Look! It's a lion.
20.	Oops!	Realization / making a mistake	Oops! Sorry I didn't notice that glass plate.

Though we are using many interjections in our normal conversation, they are bound by context. For example, the interjection *"Wow!"* is used for expressing surprise at the moment of the utterance. Without context, the listener would not know the referent of the expression (i.e., the source of the surprise). Similarly, the interjection *"Ouch!"* generally expresses pain, but it requires contextual information for the listener to determine the cause of the pain. Several English interjections contain sounds as opposed to words and they do not exist in regular phonological register.

Test yourself

Worksheet:

I. Identify the interjections in the sentences given below:

1. That was the best performance that I have ever seen, bravo!

2. Wow! You look great tonight.

3. Oh boy, we have pizza for supper!

4. Hello, Ranjan! Nice to meet you.

5. Hurray! I won the race.

II. Below is a passage from Mark Twain's "Tom Sawyer."

1. **Read the story carefully and find out any 3 interjections.**

Tom Sawyer: Chapter II

Tom went on whitewashing—paid no attention to the steamboat. Ben stared a moment and then

said: "Hi-yi! You're up a stump, ain't you!"

No answer. Tom surveyed his last touch with the eye of an artist, then he gave his brush another

gentle sweep and surveyed the result, as before. Ben ranged up alongside of him. Tom's mouth

watered for the apple, but he stuck to his work.

Ben said: "Hello, old chap, you got to work, hey?"

Tom wheeled suddenly and said: "Why, it's you, Ben! I wasn't noticing."

III. Supply the missing interjections choosing the suitable one from the brackets:

1. _____________ did you see monster truck go by?

2. _____________ *I can't believe you broke my favourite toy.*

3. _____________ J.K.Rowling is reading a book at the local library.

4. _____________ *my friend! You deserve it.*

5. _____________ I've struck gold!

(Uh oh!, Dude!, Yay!, What!, Well done!, Eureka!)

IV. Which interjection suits the blank better? Choose out of pairs:

1. _____________ I think I have lost my keys again. (a) Uh oh! (b) Yippee!

2. _____________ that was the best performance today. (a) What! (b) Bravo!

3. Don't blame me. It's your fault. _____________. (a) Er! (b) Hmph!

4. _______________ Why didn't you hold the door for me? (a) Bravo! (b) My goodness!

5. ___________________ Did I make a mistake? (a) Oh! (b) Ah!

V. Find out the errors in the usage of interjection and rewrite using the right one:

1. Ouch! I won the game.

2. Bravo! It's an insult.

3. Oops! The baby is sleeping in the other room.

4. Alas! What a great news!

5. Hi! Don't make noise in the library.

VI. Create your own sentences using the following interjections based on the situations given below:

1. Phew!

    Ididnotcompletemyassignmentbut___________________________________
    Phew!

2. My goodness!

    My   goodness!   You   have   forgotten   everything   about

    ____

3. Oops!

    Oops!   Sorry,   I   didn't   bring   my   textbook   because

    _______________________.

4. Well done!

    Well done! You achieved your dream of ____________________________.

Unit-III
COMMUNICATIVE ENGLISH

SPEAKING COMPETENCIES:

Speaking is the process of transmitting ideas and information orally in a variety of situations. (Quianthy, 1990). Effective oral communication involves generating messages and delivering them with attention to vocal variety, articulation, and non-verbal signals. In order to be a Competent Speaker, a person must be able to compose a message and provide ideas and information suitable to the topic, purpose, and audience. Specifically, the competent speaker should exhibit the competencies by demonstrating the abilities to speak effectively.

Listening is the process of receiving, constructing meaning from, and responding to spoken and or nonverbal messages. Generally people listen in order to comprehend information, critique and evaluate a message, show empathy for the feelings expressed by others, or appreciate a performance. Effective listening includes both literal and critical comprehension of ideas and information transmitted in oral language.

EMPLOY ACTIVE LISTENING TECHNIQUES WHEN APPROPRIATE:

1. Identify the cognitive and affective dimensions of a message.
2. Demonstrate comprehension by formulating questions that clarify or qualify the speaker's content and affective intent.
3. Demonstrate comprehension by paraphrasing the speaker's message.

TED Talks:

"TED" is short form for "Technology, Entertainment, Design", in fact, TED now offers much more than these three things. TED.com is an amazing resource for English learners.

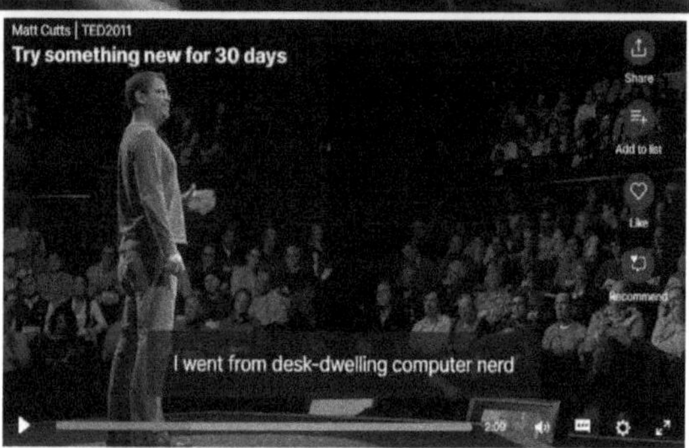

Introduction:

TED Talks are a fantastic resource for learning English. TED speakers are trained in the art of giving effective presentations through their talks. TED Talks can teach you about how to think critically about new or difficult information which is a skill that will benefit you almost immediately to have a flourishing career. Listening to experts talk or present can also help you grow as a leader by providing you with advice about how to lead others and yourself with confidence.

This chapter shows you how to get the maximum benefit from the talk by applying active listening techniques. Imagine a website that offers thousands of short talks on any topic that you can think of. The speakers are experts in their fields and know how to make their talks interesting. Now imagine that the site offers great support features, such as subtitles in various languages and ways to slow down or speed up the video. Doesn't this sound like a great tool for someone learning English? If so, there's good news. This is exactly what you will find on the TED website.

Applications for finding TED talks:

It's easy to find TED talks. The website is <u>ted.com</u>. You can view the site on your desktop or phone, as well as on apps for most major smartphones. How about watching TED talks on your TV? Apps are available for most smart TVs. You can also use a Chromecast or similar device to "cast" TED talks to your TV.If you are a fan of YouTube, you'll find that TED has a channel there.

Effectiveness of TED talks:

An effective speaker uses expressive language, such as idioms, to get their point across. They also use emphatic language to make their points stronger. (An example of emphatic language is saying "massive" instead of "very big".) This means that TED talks can introduce you to a wide range of vocabulary that you can use to be more expressive yourself.

Techniques to learn:

The basic way to use TED talks is to treat them like a simple listening exercise. You listen and, hopefully, you will learn something. But this is a passive way of learning. To be an effective, independent learner, you need to be an ACTIVE listener. This means that you need to engage with the listening materials - *analyse it, repeat it, work with it and use it yourself.*

1. **Watch the video more than once**

    An active listener knows to listen more than once. Many TED videos are three to five minutes long. This is a perfect length for watching more than once. The first time you watch a TED video, watch it for your own enjoyment. The second time you watch it, watch it to learn something about English. The first time you watch it, focus on the main ideas. The second time you watch it, focus on the details. The first time you watch it, practise note-taking by writing down the main ideas. The second time you watch it, write down useful phrases and expressions. Should you watch it more than twice? Yes, why not? As long as you are learning something, watch it as many times as you wish.

2. **Absorb new vocabulary**

Active learners know to write down new words that they hear. But this is only the first step in active listening. New vocabulary does not always mean new words. For example, you know the word GO and the word FROM. But have you heard them used like this before...? "I went from desk-dwelling computer nerd to the kind of guy who bikes to work." Do you use this phrase yourself? Could you use it in a sentence? These are the kinds of questions to ask yourself if you want to be an active learner. "After all, in a classroom, you have the teacher to ask you questions. But, as an independent learner, you have to ask those questions yourself." An active listener knows to apply this technique to grammar, too. How does the speaker use <u>modal verbs</u>? Why did he use the past continuous tense in that sentence? The important thing is to keep asking questions. These questions will help you to analyse what you hear. Interacting with the language like this is a powerful way to learn.

3. **Use the transcript feature**

Some speakers use more advanced language than others. Some speak more quickly. Should you use the transcript feature to help you understand?

Yes, absolutely. For example, you could listen once without the transcript and a second time with the transcript. It's not "cheating"!

Using the transcript can help you to focus on the speaker's language.

It can be hard to write down new words, such as "desk-dwelling" the first time you hear them (to dwell means to live or spend a lot of time somewhere). The transcript can help you do this.

Remember, an active learner makes full use of any tools that are available.

4. **Practise reading aloud**

Read the transcript aloud with the speaker to practise your pronunciation and vocal skills.

See if you can hear which words the speaker emphasises and repeats. Can you read comfortably at the same speed? Shadowing is a technique where you repeat the audio just after hearing it, like an echo.

5. **Rewrite the talk**

Practise writing while listening. Rewriting a TED talk after listening to it. Don't worry about writing exactly what you heard. Instead write your own version in a summary. Afterwards, check the transcript to see that you understood all the main points. Generally, each paragraph in the transcript covers one main point. As an active learner, you can watch, analyse and learn.

For example,

What body language does the speaker use?

What words does the speaker use to capture the audience's attention?

Pay special attention to transitional phrases, where the speaker introduces a new point. These are key to giving a good presentation (or writing a good essay).

Source: https://www.ted.com/talks

https://www.ted.com/speakers/matt_cutts

https://www.leonardoenglish.com/

Formal PowerPoint Presentation

Simple rules for better PowerPoint presentations

Have you ever given a PowerPoint presentation and noticed that something about it just seemed a little … off? If you're unfamiliar with basic PowerPoint design principles, it can be difficult to create a slide show that presents your information in the best light. Poorly designed presentations can leave an audience feeling confused, bored, and even irritated. Review these tips to make your next presentation more engaging.

Don't read your presentation straight from the slides

If your audience can both read and hear, it's a waste of time for you to simply read your slides aloud. Your audience will zone out and stop listening to what you're saying, which means they won't hear any extra information you include. Instead of typing out your entire presentation, include only main ideas, keywords, and talking points in your slide show text. Engage your audience by sharing the details out loud.

Follow the Five rule

To keep your audience from feeling overwhelmed, you should keep the text on each slide short and to the point. Some experts suggest using no more than **five** words per line of text, **five** lines of text per slide, or **five** text-heavy slides in a row.

Don't forget your audience

Humor can lighten up a presentation, but if you use it inappropriately your audience might think you don't know what you're doing. Know your audience, and tailor your presentation to their tastes and expectations.

Choose readable colors and fonts

Your text should be easy to read and pleasant to look at. Large, simple fonts and theme colors are always your best bet. The best fonts and colors can vary depending on your presentation setting.

Use animations sparingly to enhance your presentation

When used sparingly, subtle effects and animations can add to your presentation. For example, having bullet points appear as you address them rather than before can help keep your audience's attention. Keep these tips in mind when creating a presentation.

Use interesting fonts

PowerPoint's **theme fonts:** Each PowerPoint theme includes a pair of fonts—one for **headings** and **titles**, and another for **bullet points** and **paragraph text**. Including more than one font is key to making your slides look **well-designed**.

Create your own color scheme

PowerPoint themes also include premade sets of **colors**. Like the fonts pairings, many of these color sets are a little bland. Just like with theme fonts, you can also **create custom theme colors**.

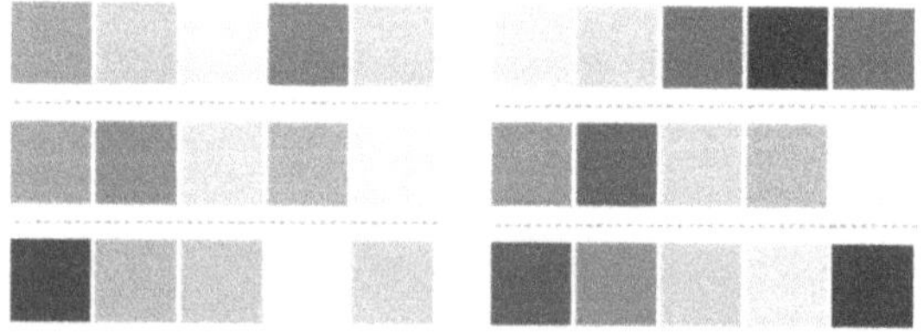

Use theme variants

Try applying a **theme variant:** Applying a theme variant changes a few minor aspects of your theme's **appearance**. Some themes have variants that are only subtly different from the original, while other themes include variants with totally different color schemes and background images.

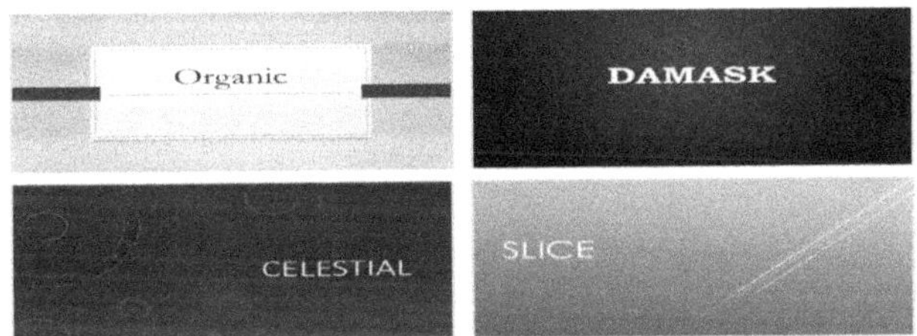

How to Interact With Audience Members During a Presentation:

1. Ask a Series of "Raise Your Hand If…" Questions

   The first simple thing to try is to ask audience a series of questions. Each question should demand a gradually-more-difficult response throughout the presentation.

   Within the first 60 seconds of a presentation, ask the audience a simple question about themselves – then get them to respond by raising their hands. Attention span during lectures showed that the first lapses in listener attention tend to happen within the first minute of the talk. So, by asking a question right away, sparks an interaction and establish a small, immediate connection.

2. Tell a Joke

   Another simple way that to forge a connection at the beginning of your presentation is by telling a joke. A joke is, in itself, a smart way to interact with audience members since it's a natural back and forth. It either asks the audience to answer a question (Why did the chicken cross the road?), or it elicits laughter (hopefully).

   Journal of Personality and Social Psychology proved that using humor improves peoples' perception in a professional setting. So try making your listeners laugh, and they'll think even more highly of you from the get-go.

3. Use a Polling Tool

    Polls are one of the best ways to interact with audience members. They cause people to think critically about what they hear and urge them to share their own opinions and expertise. Aside from the typical hand-raising poll, technology can help here. Put a question on the screen, then ask people to respond via their smartphone or laptop. There are many polling tools out there that you can use to collect responses, including Polleverywhere.com which is a popular app that can collect and broadcast poll results in real-time.

4. Get the Slides in Peoples' Hands

    Presentation Slies help communicate ideas clearly, but they can also get people to participate while speaking. Give people a closer look at slides by using a tool that can bring those slides directly into their hands.

5. Get Active

    The fact that the talk doesn't mean it has to be one-sided. Get people to interact with activities. For instance, instruct audience members to pair off, then give them 5 minutes complete an exercise. This exercise could simply be an icebreaker to get to know someone else in the room. On the other hand, it could be an exercise that helps them develop useful skills you're trying to impart (i.e. sales techniques, communication strategies, and more).

6. Create an Interactive Experience

    Goal here is to make the audience feel like they are participating in something. Have them move around the room. Create a space that doesn't feel like an auditorium or physically interact with the audience, it feels like something is happening to them.

How to Interact With Audience Members After Presentation:

Audiences typically become more receptive to a speaker's message when they trust the individual's expertise. However, delivering a presentation to an unknown audience of people personally or professionally demands great challenge. Interacting with them can help overcome this lack of familiarity and establish the credibility needed for success. For instance, interactive techniques such as responding to audience questions help show the depth of knowledge and communicates helpful intentions. By the end of a single truly interactive presentation, it is easy earn listeners' respect and have them embrace the ideas.

Greater feedback:

Receiving feedback can help become an exceptional presenter quickly by removing uncertainty about the strengths and weaknesses of delivery. Interaction through surveys or conversations with audience members can reveal what fascinated people most and what left them confused or bored. Especially if presenting the same content to multiple groups, benefit from feedback can help improve each time. However, even feedback for a onetime presentation can help identify strategies to embrace when speaking about a different topic in the future.

Enhanced professional reputation:

Giving presentations is a professional skill that many employers highly value. Whether meeting with clients or onboarding new hires, presenting can have a profound effect on business outcomes. When delivering an interactive presentations that make an impression on peers, managers or acquaintances, establishes a talented communicator who can bring value to a variety of situations

Source:

https://edu.gcfglobal.org/en/powerpoint-tips/simple-rules-for-better-powerpoint-presentations/1/

Reading and Writing

Email Writing:

Email stands for electronic mail and is a method of sending, receiving, and producing information over the internet through an electronic communication system.

Email writing is an essential part of professional communication. It is not easy to get people to respond to your emails if they do not feel interested in your message or proposal. This is exactly the reason why you should learn to write good emails. Be bold. Get to the point right away. The best email communication is the one that is simple and clear.

There are a few tips you have to keep in mind when you sit down to write emails. Emails can be casual or professional, just like informal and formal letters. The format of the email changes according to the kind of email you are writing. However, accurate grammar and spelling are aspects that are to be taken seriously.

writing an email: Steps to follow:

- Make sure you type in the right email ID. Always check with the receiver for the exact **email address** because even a full stop that is not part of the email address can land your email with the wrong person, or the mail would simply bounce.

- The **Subject** line is the next most important factor you should carefully consider because that is the first thing anyone receiving the email would see. It also determines if the receiver would want to open the mail. 'The from line is what recipients use to determine whether to delete an email. The subject line is what motivates people to actually open the email.'

said Loren McDonald. Spend double the time you spend on drafting the body to draft the subject.

- See to it that your **Salutation or Greeting** is appropriate to the receiver/s. The greeting builds a rapport.

- The **Body** of the email states what the email is about. Be clear with what you want your receiver to know. Make sure you have everything you want to convey drafted in simple terms. Do not use colloquial language or long unwinding sentences. Try not to repeat words or use cliched terms. Make your message positive, even if you're turning down an offer. If you have to follow, do it before they remind you to. Keep it short. Use standard font style and size. Do a final spelling/grammar check/proofread.

- Finally, **Sign off** the email on a polite note and proofread it before hitting send. The closing should feel genuine; only then will the receiver want to respond.

What is CC and BCC in email?

CC stands for "carbon copy." BCC stands for "blind carbon copy." When you put an email address in the CC or «carbon copy» field it means that a copy of the email you are sending will also be sent to that address.

Bcc stands for blind carbon copy which is similar to that of Cc except that **the Email address of the recipients specified in this field do not appear in the received message header and the recipients in the To or Cc fields will not know that a copy sent to these address**.

Email: Writing a complaint (Format and Samples)

From: Name and email (myname@myemailprovider.net)

Subject: (short description of your complaint)

Date: Most email programs enter this field automatically

To: (enter the email address of the person you are contacting)

CC: (local consumer group) (appropriate government agencies)

Dear (title) _____:

I wish to complain about _____ (name of product or service, with serial number or account number) that I purchased on _____ (date and location of transaction).

I am complaining because _____ (the reason you are dissatisfied). To resolve this problem I would like you to _____ (what you want the business to do).

When I first learned of this problem, I contacted _____ (name of the person, date of the call) at your company, and was told that nothing could be done about my problem. I believe that this response is unfair because _____ (the reason you feel the company has an obligation to you). I would like a written statement explaining your company's position and what you will do about my complaint.

I look forward to hearing from you as soon as possible to resolve this problem. If I do not hear from you within _____ days I will file complaints with the appropriate consumer agencies and consider my legal alternatives.

I am attaching copies of my receipt or _____________ (other proof of payment or documentation of complaint).

You may reply to me at this email or call me at (phone number).

Sincerely,

(your full name)

Sample email:

Dear Manager

Re: Complaint about faulty Television Cabinet purchased at cabinet world on 15 December 2016

I am unhappy with the quality of a television cabinet I bought at 5 Street on 15 December and I am writing to seek a replacement.

The cabinet doors do not open and shut properly and the stain on the cabinet is uneven, with one half darker than the other. The cabinet was delivered on

30 December and I noticed this problem as soon as I unpacked it from the box.

The cabinet is not of acceptable quality and does not match the sample cabinet I was shown in store. I would like you to replace it with one of the same quality and finish as the sample and arrange for return of the faulty cabinet at no cost.

I have attached a photocopy of my receipt as proof of purchase.

I would like to have this problem fixed quickly please. If I do not hear from you within 10 days, I will lodge a formal complaint with Consumer Affairs in my state.

You can contact me on 1234 5678 during working hours or after hours on 123 456 789 to discuss this matter further.

Yours sincerely,

Jane Brown

Enclosed: Copy of the receipt for television cabinet

123 Main Street
Town, TX 77008

April 12, 2021

Mark Smith
Customer Relations Director
Sofa Showroom
555 Broadway
Cityville, KS 66214

Dear Mr. Smith:

Re: Broken sofa

On March 1, 2021, I bought a sofa, model number 25811, serial number 850599-4204 at the Sofa Showroom located at 1834 Tulip Ave., Town, TX 77001. I paid $650.00 for the sofa on my credit card. Sofa Showroom delivered the sofa to my home on March 10, 2021.

Unfortunately, your product has not performed well because the sofa is defective. One of the legs broke off on March 31, 2021. The sofa is unsteady and rocks while I sit on it, so it is not comfortable or relaxing. I have not used this sofa in a way that would cause any damage. I returned to the store on April 5 and April 8, but the store manager, Aaron, would not speak to me.

To resolve the problem, I would appreciate if your company would pick up this sofa, for free, and refund the $650 I paid. Enclosed are copies of my records, including my receipt, delivery invoice, and photos of the broken sofa.

I look forward to your reply and a resolution to my problem and will wait until May 1, 2021, before seeking help from my state consumer protection office or other assistance. Please contact me at the above address or by phone at 123-456-7890.

Sincerely,

Jane Roe

Enclosure(s)

Famous Speech – Read aloud:

Reading out loud improves communication skills:

You increase your spoken word vocabulary faster when reading out loud. This is also one of the reasons why reading aloud is recommended for people who stutter when speaking. So, yes, reading aloud helps you speak better.

Benefits of Reading out Loud:

- Increases attention span. Reading a book together takes time and focused attention.
- Builds vocabulary. The more words we are exposed to, the more words we learn.
- Increases brain power.
- Relates Bonding.
- Shows that reading is important.

Read the following speech aloud to improve communication skill:

I have a dream by Martin Luther King, Jr.

I am happy to join with you today in what will go down in history as the greatest demonstration for freedom in the history of our nation. Five score years ago, a great American, in whose symbolic shadow we stand today, signed the Emancipation Proclamation. This momentous decree came as a great beacon light of hope to millions of Negro slaves who had been seared in the flames of withering injustice. It came as a joyous daybreak to end the long night of their captivity. But one hundred years later, the Negro still is not free. One hundred years later, the life of the Negro is still sadly crippled by the manacles of segregation and the chains of discrimination. One hundred years later, the Negro lives on a lonely island of poverty in the midst of a vast ocean of material prosperity. One hundred years later, the Negro is still languished in the corners of American society and finds himself an exile in his own land. And so we've come here today to dramatize a shameful condition. In a sense we've come to our nation's capital to cash a check. When the architects of our republic wrote the magnificent words of the Constitution and the Declaration of Independence, they were signing a promissory note to which every American was to fall heir. This note was a promise that all men, yes, black men as well as white men, would be guaranteed the "unalienable Rights" of "Life, Liberty and the pursuit of Happiness." It is obvious today that America has defaulted on this promissory note, insofar as her citizens of color are concerned. Instead of honoring this sacred obligation, America has given the Negro people a bad check, a check which has come back marked "insufficient funds." But we refuse to believe that the bank of justice is bankrupt. We refuse to believe that there are insufficient funds in the great vaults of opportunity of this nation. And so, we've come to cash this check, a check that will give us upon demand the riches of freedom and the security of justice. We have also come to this hallowed spot to remind America of the fierce urgency of Now. This is no time to engage in the luxury of cooling off or to take the tranquilizing drug of gradualism. Now is the time to make real the promises of democracy. Now is the time to rise from the dark and desolate valley of segregation to the sunlit path of racial justice. Now is the time to lift our nation from the quicksand's of racial injustice to the solid rock of brotherhood. Now is the time to make justice a reality for all of God's children. It would be fatal for the nation to overlook the urgency of the moment. This sweltering summer of the Negro's legitimate discontent will not pass until there is an invigorating autumn of freedom and equality. Nineteen sixty-three is not an end, but a beginning. And those who hope that the Negro needed to blow off steam and will now be content will have a rude awakening if the nation returns to business as usual. And there will be neither rest nor tranquility in

America until the Negro is granted his citizenship rights. The whirlwinds of revolt will continue to shake the foundations of our nation until the bright day of justice emerges. But there is something that I must say to my people, who stand on the warm threshold which leads into the palace of justice: In the process of gaining our rightful place, we must not be guilty of wrongful deeds. Let us not seek to satisfy our thirst for freedom by drinking from the cup of bitterness and hatred. We must forever conduct our struggle on the high plane of dignity and discipline. We must not allow our creative protest to degenerate into physical violence. Again and again, we must rise to the majestic heights of meeting physical force with soul force. The marvelous new militancy which has engulfed the Negro community must not lead us to a distrust of all white people, for many of our white brothers, as evidenced by their presence here today, have come to realize that their destiny is tied up with our destiny. And they have come to realize that their freedom is inextricably bound to our freedom. We cannot walk alone. And as we walk, we must make the pledge that we shall always march ahead. We cannot turn back. There are those who are asking the devotees of civil rights, "When will you be satisfied?" We can never be satisfied as long as the Negro is the victim of the unspeakable horrors of police brutality. We can never be satisfied as long as our bodies, heavy with the fatigue of travel, cannot gain lodging in the motels of the highways and the hotels of the cities. We cannot be satisfied as long as the negro's basic mobility is from a smaller ghetto to a larger one. We can never be satisfied as long as our children are stripped of their self-hood and robbed of their dignity by signs stating: "For Whites Only." We cannot be satisfied as long as a Negro in Mississippi cannot vote and a Negro in New York believes he has nothing for which to vote. No, no, we are not satisfied, and we will not be satisfied until "justice rolls down like waters, and righteousness like a mighty stream."[1] I am not unmindful that some of you have come here out of great trials and tribulations. Some of you have come fresh from narrow jail cells. And some of you have come from areas where your quest -- quest for freedom left you battered by the storms of persecution and staggered by the winds of police brutality. You have been the veterans of creative suffering. Continue to work with the faith that unearned suffering is redemptive. Go back to Mississippi, go back to Alabama, go back to South Carolina, go back to Georgia, go back to Louisiana, go back to the slums and ghettos of our northern cities, knowing that somehow this situation can and will be changed. Let us not wallow in the valley of despair, I say to you today, my friends. And so even though we face the difficulties of today and tomorrow, I still have a dream. It is a dream deeply rooted in the American dream. I have a dream that one day this nation will rise up and live out the true meaning of its creed: "We hold these truths to be self-evident, that all men are created equal." I have a dream that one day on the red hills of Georgia, the sons of former slaves and the sons of former slave owners will be able to sit down together at the table of brotherhood. I have a dream that one day even the state of Mississippi, a state sweltering with the heat of injustice, sweltering with the heat of oppression, will be transformed into an oasis of freedom and justice. I have a dream that my four little children will one day live in a nation where they will not be judged by the color of their skin but by the content of their character. I have a dream today! I have a dream that one day, down in Alabama, with its vicious racists, with its governor having his lips dripping with the words of "interposition" and "nullification" -- one day right there in Alabama little black boys and black girls will be able to join hands with little white boys and white girls as sisters and brothers. I have a dream today! I have a dream that one day every valley shall be exalted, and every hill and mountain shall be made low, the rough places will be made plain, and the crooked places will be made straight; "and the glory of the Lord shall be revealed and all flesh shall see it together."2 This is our hope, and this is the faith that I go back to the South with. With this faith, we will be able to hew out of the mountain of despair a stone of hope. With this faith, we will be able to transform the jangling discords of our nation into a beautiful symphony of brotherhood. With this faith, we will be able to work together, to pray together, to struggle together, to go to jail together, to stand up for freedom together, knowing that we will be free one day. And this will be the day -- this will be the day when all of God's children will be able to sing with new meaning: My country 'tis of thee, sweet land of liberty, of thee I sing. Land where my fathers died, land of the Pilgrim's pride, From every mountainside, let freedom ring! And if America is to be a great nation, this must become true. And so let freedom ring from the prodigious hilltops of New Hampshire. Let freedom ring from the mighty mountains of New York. Let freedom ring from the heightening Alleghenies of Pennsylvania. Let freedom ring from the snow-capped Rockies of Colorado. Let freedom ring from the curvaceous slopes of California. But not only that: Let freedom ring from Stone Mountain of Georgia. Let freedom ring from Lookout Mountain of Tennessee. Let freedom ring from every hill and molehill of Mississippi. From every mountainside, let freedom ring. And when this happens, when we allow freedom ring, when we let it ring from every village and every hamlet, from every state and every city, we will be able to speed up that day when all of God's children, black men and white men, Jews and Gentiles, Protestants and Catholics, will be able to join hands and sing in the words of the old Negro spiritual: Free at last! Free at last! Thank God Almighty, we are free at last!

Reading from famous pieces of literature: (Try reading with intonation)

a) Hamlet, 'To be, or not to be' soliloquy.

To be, or not to be, that is the question:

Whether 'tis nobler in the mind to suffer

The slings and arrows of outrageous fortune,

Or to take arms against a sea of troubles

And by opposing end them. To die—to sleep,

No more; and by a sleep to say we end

The heart-ache and the thousand natural shocks

That flesh is heir to: 'tis a consummation

Devoutly to be wish'd. To die, to sleep;

To sleep, perchance to dream—ay, there's the rub:

For in that sleep of death what dreams may come,

When we have shuffled off this mortal coil,

Must give us pause—there's the respect

That makes calamity of so long life…

b)   Mark Antony, 'Friends, Romans, countrymen' speech from *Julius Caesar*.

Friends, Romans, countrymen, lend me your ears;

I come to bury Caesar, not to praise him.

The evil that men do lives after them;

The good is oft interred with their bones;

So let it be with Caesar. The noble Brutus

Hath told you Caesar was ambitious:

If it were so, it was a grievous fault,

And grievously hath Caesar answer'd it.

Here, under leave of Brutus and the rest–

For Brutus is an honourable man;

So are they all, all honourable men–

Come I to speak in Caesar's funeral.

He was my friend, faithful and just to me:

But Brutus says he was ambitious;

And Brutus is an honourable man …

c)   Jacques, 'Seven Ages of Man' speech from *As You Like It*.

All the world's a stage,

And all the men and women merely players:

They have their exits and their entrances;

And one man in his time plays many parts,

His acts being seven ages. At first the infant,

Mewling and puking in the nurse's arms.

And then the whining school-boy, with his satchel

And shining morning face, creeping like snail

Unwillingly to school. And then the lover,

Sighing like furnace, with a woeful ballad

Made to his mistress' eyebrow. Then a soldier,

Full of strange oaths and bearded like the pard,

Jealous in honour, sudden and quick in quarrel,

Seeking the bubble reputation

Even in the cannon's mouth ...

Preparing Short Assignment

Short Assignment: The main feature of short assignment / essay writing is that students must put all their ideas and arguments into a limited amount of space. Usually, short assignments take between 200 and 500 words, depending on the topic and teacher's requirements.

Here's a quick overview of the five important stages of an assignment that will help you tackle your first one.

Plan and prepare. The first stage of an assignment is all about planning. Check the criteria, brainstorm your initial ideas, ask any questions early and determine the purpose and direction of your argument. Write a plan that you can refer back to.

Research and take notes. This can often be the most time-consuming stage, but it is a necessary task. Ask the library to help you find the sources you need and take detailed notes. This is also a good time to check which referencing style you have to follow for your assignment.

Write the first draft. Your first draft should get your ideas on paper into a coherent order – your sentences don't have to be perfect.

Revise and re-draft. Read guide to drafting, and allocate time to checking that you have referenced your sources correctly.

Proofread and submit. Now is the time to print out your assignment and get out the red pen! Remember to also read the submission requirements in your unit guide, use Turnitin, and then submit it and do a celebratory dance.

ASSIGNMENT WRITING

THE BASIC STRUCTURAL ELEMENTS OF YOUR ASSIGNMENTS ARE:		
1. **COVER PAGE**	4.	**MAIN TEXT/BODY**
2. **CONTENTS PAGE**	5.	**CONCLUSION**
3. **INTRODUCTION**	6.	**REFERENCES**

THE COVER PAGE

Students may design their own cover page (selection of different fonts, addition of graphics etc.) . However, the minimum information that must be on your cover page is shown below.

The Introduction:

Tells the reader what the assignment is going to be about.

- Provides the reader with the necessary background for what is to follow (i.e. a set of signposts).

Main Text/Body:

- Tells the reader what the paper is about.

- Should contain a logical development of the argument.

- Write to a predetermined plan and structure.

- Gradually build up your case.

- Keep your focus on the problem; don't get side tracked.

- Be critical and analytical in your approach.

Conclusion or Recommendation

- Reminds the reader what the paper has been about.

- Should be precise and straightforward.

- Make sure your argument in the body of the assignment supports your conclusion.

Word Power

Word Power uses a contextual approach to instruction (teaching words in the context of high-quality texts). Word Power provides pupils with the specific skills they need to strengthen in order to Power-Up word knowledge, helping to take the mystery out of vocabulary instruction. Word Power is not a 'word of the day' resource, but rather a practical tool to help pupils learn how to tackle everyday words they will encounter when reading and listening (receptive language), writing and speaking (expressive language).

One-Word Substitution:

Complete the following sentences using an appropriate word. Choose your answers from the given options.

1. *It was such a .... state of affairs that we had to laugh.*

    comic

    categorical

    brazen

2. *The senator's .... made him intolerant of other countries.*

    brashness

    stupidity

    chauvinism

3.   The teacher .... the child for arriving late.

chastised

reprimanded

censured

All of the above

4.   Without rules, people would live in a state of ....

chaos

harmony

bungle

5.   The minister made a .... denial of the charges that he had taken bribes.

brazen

categorical

brash

6.   The plumber .... the job and now the pipe leaks.

bungled

abashed

chastised

7.   How can you believe such a .... lie?

brazen

white

sordid

8.   Buying the house without having it appraised was ....

brazen

brash

impudent

9. *It is important to .... with those in trouble to really understand their suffering.*

   empathize

   emote

   devise

10. *The spy checked into the hotel under a .... name.*

    figurative

    fictitious

    alien

Answers

1. It was such a **comic / comical** state of affairs that we had to laugh.
2. The senator's **chauvinism** made him intolerant of other countries.
3. The teacher **chastised** the child for arriving late.
4. Without rules, people would live in a state of **chaos.**
5. The minister made a **categorical** denial of the charges that he had taken bribes.
6. The plumber **bungled** the job and now the pipe leaks.
7. How can you believe such a **brazen** lie?
8. Buying the house without having it appraised was **brash.**

Meanings

Comic / comical – funny, humorous, laughable

Chauvinism – super patriotism

Chastise – punish, reprimand, scold

Chaos – turmoil, upheaval, confusion

Categorical – absolute, unconditional

Bungle – do badly, make a mess of

Brazen – impudent, shameless

Brash – rash, reckless, careless

Source: https://blog.pobble.com/word-power-a-unique-approach-to-vocabulary-learning

Exercise 2

ACROSS

1. One who is present everywhere
4. One who goes on foot
6. One who can do anything for money
7. One who hates mankind
8. One who thinks only of himself
9. One who works for free
15. One who does not make mistakes
16. One who lives in a foreign country.
17. One who eats too much
18. One who looks on the dark side of things
19. One who believes in fate

DOWN

2. One who loves mankind
3. One who doubts the existence of god
5. One who pretends to be what he is not
10. One who is easily deceived
11. One who is all-powerful
12. One who looks on the bright side of things
13. One who thinks only of welfare of women .
14. One who is unable to walk normally

WORD BANK: Agnostic, egoist, fatalist, feminist, glutton, gullible, hypocrite, immigrant, infallible, lame, mercenary, misanthrope, omnipotent, omnipresent, optimist, pedestrian, pessimist, philanthropist, volunteer.

Solution:

GRAMMAR IN CONTEXT - SENTENCE PATTERN

Basic sentence pattern in English:

In English, sentences usually operate using a similar pattern: subject, verb, then object. The nice part about this type of structure is that it lets reader easily know who is doing the action and what the outcome of the action is.

A **subject** performs the action in a sentence.

- For instance, in the sentence, "Matt eats pizza," *Matt* is the subject because he is the one eating the pizza.

    A **verb** is a word that usually indicates some type of action. There are two basic types of verbs in English: **action verbs** and

linking verbs. An action verb represents something the subject of a sentence does, whereas a linking verb connects the subject to a specific state of being. In other words, a linking verb describes a subject instead of expressing an action. Linking verbs are also known at **state of being verbs**, and the most common one in English is the verb *to be*.

- If we consider the above sentence, "Matt eats pizza," the verb is *eats*, which is an action verb because it tells us what Matt does – he eats.

- In this sentence, "Matt is hungry," our verb *is*, which is a form of *to be*, a linking verb. Notice how Matt does not do anything in this sentence. Instead, the verb *is* describes how Matt feels – hungry. *Is* links Matt with hunger.

  An **object** usually appears after the verb. There are two types of objects in the English language: **direct** and **indirect**.

- A direct object takes or receives the action of the verb. In other words, the subject of the sentence acts on the direct object.

  ○ The direct object in our sample sentence "Matt eats pizza" is pizza. Matt eats what? Pizza.

  An **indirect object** tells us to whom or for whom an action is done. To understand this concept, we need to come up with a longer sentence.

- Our new sample sentence will be, "Matt cuts the pizza for Nate." In this sentence, our subject is Matt, our verb is *cuts*, the direct object is *the pizza*, and our indirect object is *Nate*. The pizza is cut for whom? Nate because Matt cuts the pizza for him.

So, remember, this is the basic pattern of an English sentence: SUBJECT + VERB + OBJECT.

Sentence Patterns	Examples
Subject + Verb	The bell rang. He wept.
Subject + Verb + Object	She likes eggs. I met my brother.
Subject + Verb + Adjective	Martin is busy. She was sick.
Subject + Verb + Adverb	The truck came here. He ran fast.
Subject + Verb + Noun	They are teachers. Marilyn was the class president.

Types Of Sentence Patterns

Look at 5 patterns in the English language.

Pattern 1 - Subject + Verb

Example:

Pradeep waltzed onto the dancefloor.

She read.

The tired old woman cleaned often.

Pattern 2 - Subject + Verb + Direct Object

Example:

Paul bought a new dress.

She read the book.

The old woman cleaned the drapes.

Pattern 3 - Subject + Verb + Direct Object + Indirect Object

Example:

Peter bought her sister a new dress.

The old woman gave the pharmacy her prescription.

Pattern 4 - Subject + Linking Verb + Noun Complement

Example:

Miriam was the class president.

The boys were boy scouts.

Pattern 5 - Subject + Linking Verb + Adjective Complement

Example:

The house is very old.

I am very hungry.

Sentence Pattern :

Subject S - The doer of the action.

Verb V - The action term.

Object O - Answers the question.

What? – Direct Object

Whom? – Indirect Object Complement

C - Completes the meaning of the sentence.

Adjunct A - Answers to the questions - How? When?, Where?

The five basic patterns are:

1. SV (Subject + Verb)

2. SVO (Subject + Verb + Object)

3. SVIODO (Subject + Verb + Indirect Object + Direct Object)

4. SVC (Subject + Verb + Complement)

5. SVOC (Subject + Verb + Object + Complement)

Note: Adjunct could be added to all these five patterns.

Exercises for practice:

Identify the pattern of the following sentences:

1. He bought his girlfriend a ring.

2. She sings and dances.

3. He made the problem complicated.

4. She goes to school.

5. John and Marry are swimming.

6. He brought me a cup of tea.

7. The company has been very successful.

8. They are in class.

9. He is brave.

10. I called my dog Poho.

Answers:

1. SV-IO-DO

2. SV

3. SV-DO-OC

4. SVA

5. SV

6. SV-IO-DO

7. SVC

8. SVA

9. SVC

10. SV-DO-OC

Source:https://academicguides.waldenu.edu/writingcenter/grammar/sentencestructure

Unit-IV
COMMUNICATIVE ENGLISH II

Importance of Listening and Speaking

Communication skills comprise receptive skills and productive skills. Listening and reading are receptive skills while speaking and writing are productive skills. Receptive skills are these in which students receive and process the information but do not need to produce a language to do this, while productive skills require the production, for instance, a speech.

Listening, is the skill of understanding spoken language. Listening is an essential skill, present in most of the activities throughout our lives. We listen to a wide variety of things, for example; what someone says during a conversation, face to face or on the telephone; announcements giving information, for example, at an airport or railway station; the weather forecast on the radio; a play on the radio; music.

Besides, Listening is a complex process due to its double psychological and social nature: Listening is a psychological phenomenon, which takes place on a cognitive level inside people's heads, and a social phenomenon which develops interactively between people and the environment surrounding them. It considers listening as a complex process, which needs to be understood in order to teach it, and subsequently, evaluate it before integrating it with phonological aspects and with the skill of speaking.

Know the difference between Listening and Hearing. So, for an effective listening stay focussed.

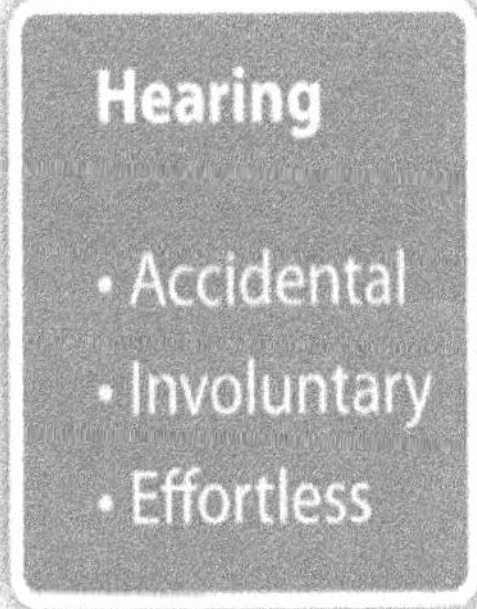

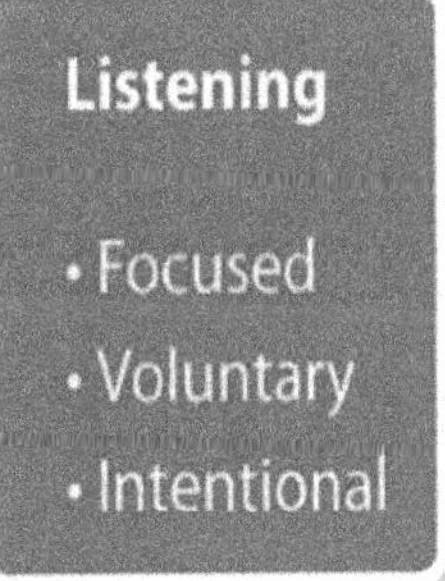

Listening, on the other hand, is purposeful and focused rather than accidental. As a result, it requires motivation and effort. Listening, at its best, is active, focused, concentrated attention for the purpose of understanding the meanings expressed by a speaker.

Hearing is an accidental and automatic brain response to sound that requires no effort. We are surrounded by sounds most of the time. For example, we are accustomed to the sounds of airplanes, lawn mowers, furnace blowers, the rattling of pots and pans, and so on. We hear those incidental sounds and, unless we have a reason to do otherwise, we train ourselves to ignore them

Participating in a meeting: Face to Face and Online

A face-to-face meeting:

A face-to-face meeting is one where all the participants are physically in the same place. In other words, a face-to-face meeting is what everyone used to just call "a meeting" before the advent of conference calls and web conferencing. Now, meetings can be characterized as face-to-face (with everyone colocated), virtual (with most all participants joining from separate locations), or hybrid (some participants colocated, others joining from different locations).

Participating in a face to face meeting:

Meeting people face to face helps you analyze micro-behaviors like body language, facial expressions, and eye contact. Simple nonverbal communication may help you judge how involved other people are in the discussion and provide insight into how they feel.

- Show Up on Time.

- Introduce Yourself and Others.

- Practice Active Listening.

- Dress Professionally & Present Well.

- Ask Questions at the Right Time.

- Speak Loudly and Clearly.

Face to face meetings is key to building strong relationships. The customer or client will feel as if they have connected with you better if you meet with them in person over communication via email or phone

Advantages of face to face meetings:

1. Face to face meetings improve communication.

2. Meeting in-person helps you to build trust and create strong business relationships.

3. Face to face meetings are more productive and have less distractions.

4. Meeting in the real world removes the possibility of connectivity issues.

5. Face to face meetings are better for collaboration, brainstorming and creativity.

6. It is easier to resolve disputes and problems when you meet face to face.

7. Traveling to (and from) a meeting can be an advantage.

Online Meeting:

What's an online meeting?

An online meeting uses audio and optional video conferencing between two or more participants. In these meetings, video provides the benefit of being able to see the expressions and reactions of other people in addition to being able to hear what they're saying. Online meetings are also commonly referred to as virtual meetings, video meetings, and web conferences.

Why are virtual meetings useful?

Virtual meetings are more important than ever before as many companies switch to hybrid work models. In a hybrid work model, employees work some days in person at their office and some days at home or from another remote location, such as a coworking space.

Benefits of online meetings include:

- **The ability to join team meetings from nearly anywhere.**

  Whether a person is at home, in the office, or out and about, virtual meetings help ensure that you never miss an important meeting, even if you can't be physically present.

- **Stronger co-worker relationships.**

  When a person is a hybrid or fully remote employee, the face time and relationship building that evolves naturally in the office can be harder to come by. But video meetings allow you to see and interact with co-workers face to face, which leads to more natural conversation, collaboration, and trust.

- **Different ways to engage.**

  Thorough virtual meeting software combines typical online meeting features, like audio and video, with additional features, like a running chat log, a hand-raising feature, and different virtual reactions to cheer on presenting co-workers.

Listening with courtesy and adding ideas and giving opinions during the meeting and making concluding remarks:

Effective communication is an essential part of a successful business. On any given day, a person is likely to communicate with employees, partners, suppliers and customers, so it's important to know how to get your message across while being courteous. Being polite and taking other people's feelings into account can reduce arguments, misunderstandings and miscommunication.

What Is Courtesy in Business Communication?

Courtesy is one of the 7 C's of communication, along with concise, clear, correct, concrete, complete and coherent. Courtesy in business communication involves showing respect to others in the workplace. This means that people need to be sincere and polite through written or in-person communication. Focus on the person communicating and listen to what they're saying to take their opinions and feelings into consideration.

Courtesy in business communication builds strong relationships in the workplace. You can gain the trust of your employees and customers by showing them respect. In addition, they learn to be courteous to you in return, which creates a welcoming and nurturing work environment.

Leading by Example in Different Situations:

Be courteous in all your business communications, which may include:

- **One-on-one conversations:** Listen carefully to the person you're speaking with and make eye contact. Refrain from multitasking, such as browsing on your computer during the conversation, so that you can give them your full attention.

- **Group meetings:** Show courtesy by being prepared for the meeting. Review agenda items, bring necessary notes and participate in the discussion. When assigning tasks, saying please and thank you goes a long way.

- **Emails:** Answer emails promptly so that people aren't left waiting for information. Address the person you're contacting by name and ensure you spell it correctly. Take time to review your email to prevent errors. Consider how your tone may sound to the reader.

- **Instant messages:** Keep in mind that this channel is for short and simple conversations. Keep your communication partner's time in mind; this isn't the best method for in-depth discussions. Use proper spelling and grammar to avoid confusion.

- **Phone calls:** Having a polite voice message for times when you're not able to pick up the phone. Return the call as soon as possible and apologize for not being able to speak to the caller earlier.

- **Video calls:** Point your camera directly at your face so that the meeting participants can see you. Avoid checking emails or your phone during the meeting to provide your full attention.

- **Formal written communications:** Review your written communication for spelling mistakes and errors and deliver your communication in a form that is accessible to your audience.

- **Customer communications:** When dealing with customers, remember that effective customer service is related to effective communication. Being polite, respectful, empathetic and understanding is essential.

Developing Guidelines for Employees

To improve business communications in your workplace, create a set of guidelines that specify why being courteous is important. Define what courteous communication looks like in your business by providing specific examples for different types of everyday interactions. For example, if your company has a large customer service component, specify how employees should deal with customers in both positive and negative situations. If your business has an extensive partner network, provide guidelines on how to conduct business with those stakeholders. Include these guidelines in your onboarding materials for all employees.

Being courteous doesn't come naturally for all people, so Prezi suggests using role-playing scenarios to help employees understand best practices and missteps. This can be part of training on effective communication where you stress the importance of respect and politeness in the workplace. Conducting regular training sessions results in employees who understand the guidelines and how to put them into practice.

25 PHRASES FOR EXPRESSING OPINIONS: I think.... I believe.... I feel.... I suppose.... I guess.... According to me.... In my view.... In my opinion.... In my eyes.... It seems to me that.... From my perspective.... From my point of view.... From my view point.... As far as I'm concerned.... Personally, I think.... I'd like to point out that.... What I mean is.... Generally it is thought that.... Some people say that.... Well, it is considered that.... It is generally accepted that.... My impression is that.... It goes without saying that.... I hold the view that.... I'm of the opinion that...

Conclusion:

Just as a good introduction helps bring an audience member into the world of your speech, and a good speech body holds the audience in that world, a good conclusion helps bring that audience member back to the reality outside of your speech.

The first thing a good conclusion can do is to signal the end of a speech. You may be thinking that showing an audience that you're about to stop speaking is a "no brainer," but many speakers really don't prepare their audience for the end. When a speaker just suddenly stops speaking, the audience is left confused and disappointed. Instead, we want to make sure that audiences are left knowledgeable and satisfied with our speeches.

Reading and Writing

Reading visual texts – advertisements:

What is a Visual Text?

The basic definition of visual literacy is the ability to read, write and create visual images. Both static and moving. It is a concept that relates to art and design but it also has much wider applications. Visual literacy is about language, communication and interaction. Visual media is a linguistic tool with which we communicate, exchange ideas and navigate our highly visual digital world. The term was first coined in 1969 by John Debes, who was the founder of the International Visual Literacy Association:

What is the purpose of visual text?

In the world today, visual texts are used **to convey messages and communicate ideas in a variety of ways**. These texts include print media such as posters and flyers as well as non-print ones like websites and online advertisements.

Visual Literacy Clues: What Are They and How Do We Read Them?

"Visual Literacy is the ability to construct meaning from images. It's not a skill. It uses skills as a toolbox. It's a form of critical thinking that enhances your intellectual capacity."

If visual literacy is about decoding meaning from images of various kinds, this process follows three general steps:

1. What Can You See?

To answer this, students must become familiar with Visual Literacy Clues (VLCs). When students are familiar with these clues they will have a method of approaching any image with a view to decoding its meaning. The VLCs are: subject matter, colors, angles, symbols vectors, lighting, gaze, gestures, and shapes. These categories provide an approach to examine the details of the various aspects of the image they are reading.

2. How Does It Make You Feel?

After the students have had time to note what they can see in the image through examination of the VLCs, it is now time for them to consider their emotional response to what they have viewed.

With close reference to the VLCs they have previously identified, students express how the image makes them feel and how it has influenced them to feel this way. They may feel anger, anguish, excitement, happy etc. There is no limit to the emotions they may refer to, provided they can point to evidence from the image. Here are some suggested questions to help the students explore their responses:

Subject Matter: What is the topic of the movie? Who and what are in the image? What is the image about?

Color: How is color used in the image? What effect do the colors chosen have on the viewer?

Angles: Are we looking from above or below? What is the camera angle? How does this affect what we see and how we feel about it?

Symbols: What symbols are used in this image? What do you think they represent? Are the colors that were chosen symbolic?

Vectors: Can you see the major lines in the image? Are they broken or unbroken? How do the lines create reading paths for our eyes?

Lighting: Can you describe the lighting used in the movie. How does it affect the 'mood' of the movie?

Gaze: What type of look is the character giving? Where is their gaze directed? What does this say?

Gesture: What type of gestures is the character giving? What is communicated by these gestures?

Shapes: What geometric shapes can you recognize in the image? Do they repeat? Is there a pattern? Is order or chaos conveyed?

3. **What is the Image trying to tell us?**

This third aspect peels back another level of meaning to get to the overall message underlying the image. This question asks the students to delve into the intentions of the image-maker themselves. The genre of the image will be of significance here too, as the student considers the nature of the image as art, entertainment, advertisement or a fusion of the various genres.

ACTIVITIES FOR THE TEACHING OF VISUAL LITERACY IN THE CLASSROOM

1. **Caption a Photograph**

Photographs are one of the most familiar forms of visual media for our students. Often photographs they see will be accompanied by captions.

In this exercise, give out copies of a single photograph to the class without captions. Their task here is to closely examine the photograph, either individually or in small groups, before writing a caption to accompany the photograph. When students have completed their captions they can compare their captions with each other before you reveal the true nature of the photograph.

Prior to writing their caption, you may wish to provide some supporting questions or background information. However, they can go in blind to any background other than what they can infer from the photograph itself.

The purpose of this activity is to reveal to the students how to interpretation a single visual image. The students will gain awareness of the power of a caption to frame an image's meaning, even if the caption is not accurate.

Some suggested questions for students to consider for Activities:

* What people, objects, or activities can you see in the picture?
* Are there any clues to when it was taken? What was happening at this time in history?
* Are there any clues to where it was taken? Are there any clues to why it was taken or who took it?
* Is it a posed photograph? A natural scene? A documentary photograph? A selfie?

Extension:

This activity can be considered as a lead-in to a bigger topic, as it can make for a great introduction to draw out the students' background knowledge and lead into a larger discussion or research project. This activity can also be easily adapted for a wide range of different types of images, for example, advertisements.

(**Source:** https://literacyideas.com/teaching-visual-texts-in-the-classroom/)

Purpose in Visual Texts:

Similar to a written text, a visual text is also created for a purpose. Some of the more common purposes include to inform, to entertain and to persuade. Look at the different visual texts and the specific purposes behind their creation:

1. **To inform**

    Some visual texts are created with the aim of disseminating information. One such text is the newsletter as its purpose is to provide factual and accurate information that is undisputable on a regular basis. Sometimes, a newsletter serves to educate the public on vital information that comes from the government, for instance the REACH Bytes E-newsletter (link: https://www.reach.gov.sg/).

    Other texts that can be used to increase awareness of specific issues include posters, notices, flyers, brochures and webpages. An example would be a flyer about how smoking is illegal at public areas like bus stops and taxi stands. This serves as an informative flyer to educate and remind the public about acts that break the law and the consequences that may be served to those who break it.

2. **To persuade**

    These visual texts want readers to take action, for instance, to get them to watch a movie, take part in an activity or attend an event. Such texts include reviews, testimonials, brochures and posters. An example would be a brochure about a newly built university to showcase its campus and the courses it offers to potential undergraduates who are seeking to enrich themselves with more knowledge and obtain a degree.

3. To advertise

Some visual texts promote a service, product or even an organisation. These usually include but are not limited to flyers, posters, advertisements as well as brochures. Such texts usually include colourful images and persuasive language aimed at attracting the readers to buy the product or service being advertised.

4. To instruct

Visual texts like recipe books and instruction manuals fall in this category. They contain important steps with accompanying pictures to teach readers how to do something, like how to bake a cake or repair a car. The textbooks of different subjects in school are excellent examples of such a text.

How to Answer Purpose-Related Questions

A type of question that is often asked for visual text comprehension is related to purpose, for example, take a look at this poster (& Habits of highly hygienic people)

1.   What is the objective of this poster?

2.   What does this brochure aim to achieve?

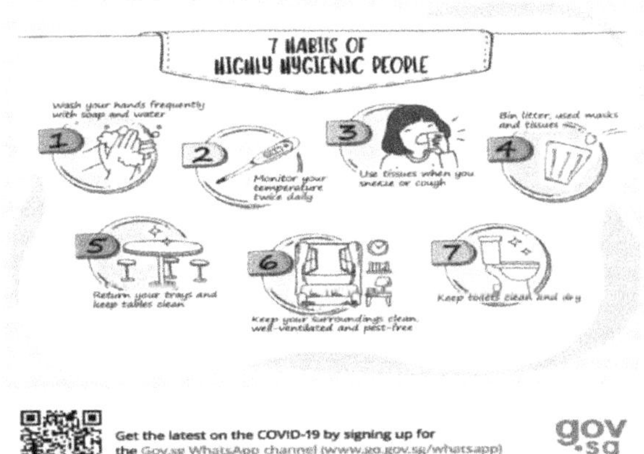

(https://lilbutmightyenglish.com/blog/understanding-purpose-related-questions-in-visual-text-comprehension/)

Preparing First Draft of Assignment

First Draft:

A good first draft can almost always be improved by revision, editing, and rewriting. As you learn to evaluate your own writing more critically, you will be able to improve it. The following checklists will help guide you from a good first draft to an improved, refined final draft.

Purpose, audience, and tone are the elements that deal with the overall effect of your essay and guide you throughout your writing.

Writing a First Draft

1. Every essay or paper is made up of three parts:

    *   Introduction

    *   Body

    *   Conclusion

2. The introduction is the first paragraph of the paper. It often begins with a general statement about the topic and ends with a more specific statement of the main idea of your paper. The purpose of the introduction is to:

    *   let the reader know what the topic is

    *   inform the reader about your point of view

    *   arouse the reader's curiosity so that he or she will want to read about your topic

3. The body of the paper follows the introduction. It consists of a number of paragraphs in which you develop your ideas in detail.

    *   Limit each paragraph to one main idea. (Don't try to talk about more than one idea per paragraph.)

    *   Prove your points continually by using specific examples and quotations from your note cards.

- Use transition words to ensure a smooth flow of ideas from paragraph to paragraph.

4. The conclusion is the last paragraph of the paper. Its purpose is to

  - summarize your points, leaving out specific examples

  - restate the main idea of the paper

(Source:https://www.infoplease.com/homework-help/writing-grammar/how-write-research-paper-4)

Introduction: (Samples)

This is an example of a poor introduction:

In 1492, Columbus set sail from Spain on a quest to find a new trade route to Asia. Despite the fact that he believed he had landed in the East Indies, Columbus had found another continent entirely. This essay will examine the issue of whether or not indigenous culture was completely decimated in the Americas as a result of Spain's colonisation in the 16th century. It will look at the areas of family, religion and language.

This is an example of a good introduction:

Beginning in the sixteenth century, Spanish colonisation of the Americas had a significantly negative effect on the cultural practices of the indigenous population. In particular, the introduction of new diseases and the consequent demographic collapse dramatically weakened indigenous culture and their ability to resist Spanish domination. However, aspects of the culture of some indigenous groups survived and even thrived—it was not completely decimated. Through an examination of the evidence related to religion, family and language, including the effects of colonisation on these areas of society, this essay will demonstrate aspects of indigenous beliefs, customs and practices that managed to endure.

In the example of a poor introduction, background information is included that is not directly relevant to the topic. Also, it does not answer the question, it only introduces it. Finally, it does not introduce all the topics to be discussed (as outlined in the final essay plan), and for those it does introduce, it does not mention them in the order they will be discussed in the essay (as outlined in the final essay plan).

By contrast, the good introduction provides a clear thesis statement; introduces, in order, all the topics to be discussed; and only includes information that is directly relevant to the essay question.

Topic sentences

The topic sentence introduces the new topic about to be discussed. It also links the topic back to the essay question, to make it clear why it is relevant and how it advances the argument.

Paragraphs

Essay plan should clearly indicate what information will go in each paragraph of the essay. Each paragraph should contain only one main idea.

Conclusions

A conclusion should restate the thesis statement and summarise the points that were made in the body of the essay in the order in which they were made. The conclusion offers an important opportunity to synthesise the points you have made to support your argument and to reinforce how these points prove that your argument is correct.

Referencing

It is important to acknowledge the sources of information in academic writing. This allows to clearly show how the ideas of others have influenced the own work. Provide a citation (and matching reference) in every time when using words, ideas or information from other sources. In this way, accidental plagiarism can be avoided.

(Source:https://www.capstoneediting.com.au/resources/how-to-write-the-first-draft)

Word Power

What are Connotation and Denotation?

Connotation and denotation are two ways of looking at the same word. The **denotation** of a word refers to the dictionary definition of its meaning. The **connotation** of a word refers to the emotion or feeling that is evoked by a word and accompanies its literal meaning.

Denotation Definition

What is the denotation of a word?

The term denotation comes from the Latin *denotationem*, meaning to note or make a note. Its contemporary definition is the literal meaning of a word as one would find in a dictionary.

Denotation Examples:

While many words have multiple meanings, the following use the primary dictionary definition for each word:

- Example 1: Quirk (n.) a peculiar trait
- Example 2: Oddity (n.) an odd person, thing, event, or trait
- Example 3: Dwelling (n.) a shelter (such as a house) in which people live
- Example 4: Home (n.) one's place of residence

Connotation Examples:

The pairs of examples below have very similar denotations as outlined in the previous section. Their connotations, however, are quite different.

- Examples 1 & 2: *Quirk* and *Oddity* both mean, in terms of their denotations, an odd or peculiar trait. The connotation of the word *quirk* is relatively positive in that the trait is perceived as cute or socially acceptable. The connotation of the word *oddity* is more negative, with the feeling that the trait is less socially acceptable.

- Examples 3 & 4: *Dwelling* and *Home* both literally mean a place where people live. The connotation of the term *dwelling* is neutral or slightly negative as it has feeling of being just a structure; empty or cold. One does not feel an attachment to a dwelling. The connotation for *home*, however, is positive in nature. The term home evokes a feeling of warmth and belonging.

Connotations and Denotations

Connotations	Denotations
The connotation of a word is a feeling or an idea associated with the word.	The denotation of a word is its literal meaning.

Examples

Denotation

Not the same

Negative Connotation	Neutral Connotation	Positive Connotation
Strange	Different	Unique

Denotation

Busy doing something

Negative Connotation	Neutral Connotation	Positive Connotation
Hyperactive	Active	Energetic

Source:https://www.tutoringhour.com/files/positive-negative-connotations/identifying.pdf

Worksheet Exercise for Practice:

Connotation Practice

Words with similar dictionary meanings often have different connotations, so it is very important for a writer to choose words carefully. Consider the following table. Each row contains a list of words with similar dictionary meanings but different shades of feeling.

	Neutral	Favorable (Positive)	Unfavorable (Negative)
1.	Inactive		
2.	Shy		
3.	Funny		
4.	Old		
5.	Reserved		
6.	Persistent		
7.	New		
8.	Conservative		
9.	Proud		
10.	Curious		

Answer Key:

Neutral	Favorable	Unfavorable
inactive	relaxed	lazy
shy	modest	mousy
funny	Good-humored	sarcastic
old	time-tested	out-of-date
reserved	dignified	stiff-necked
persistent	persevering	stubborn
new	up-to-date	newfangled
conservative	thrifty	miserly
proud	self-confident	conceited
curious	inquisitive	nosy

Source:https://www.troup.org/userfiles/929/My%20Files/ELA/MS%20
ELA/6th%20ELA/6th%20Unit%203/ConnotationActivitiesassignmentspractice.
pdf?id=21743

Grammar in Context: Sentence Types

Types of sentence based on structure:

The other way to categorize sentences is to classify them based on their structure. Each of the types of sentences discussed above also fits into the categories discussed below.

Simple sentences:

A simple sentence is the most basic type of sentence. This kind of sentence consists of just one independent clause, which means it communicates a complete thought and contains a subject and a verb.

A few examples of simple sentences include:

- How are you?
- She built a garden.
- We found some sea glass.

A simple sentence is the smallest possible grammatically correct sentence. Anything less is known as a sentence fragment.

Complex sentences:

In contrast to a simple sentence, a complex sentence contains one independent clause and at least one dependent clause. While an independent clause can be its own sentence, a dependent clause can't. Dependent clauses rely on the independent clauses in their sentences to provide context.

Dependent clauses appear after a conjunction or marker word or before a comma. Marker words are words like whenever, although, since, while, and before. These words illustrate relationships between clauses.

The following are examples of complex sentences:

- Before you enter my house, take off your shoes.

- Matt plays six different instruments, yet never performs in public.

Compound sentences:

Compound sentences are sentences that contain two or more independent clauses. In a compound sentence, the clauses are generally separated by either a comma paired with a coordinating conjunction or a semicolon. In some cases, they can be separated by a colon.

Examples of compound sentences include:

- I was thirsty, so I drank water.

- She searched through her entire closet; she could not find her denim jacket.

Compound-complex sentences:

When a sentence has two or more independent clauses *and* at least one dependent clause, that sentence is a compound-complex sentence. These are long sentences that communicate a significant amount of information. The clauses don't need to be in any specific order; as long as you've got at least two independent clauses and at least one dependent clause, you've got a compound-complex sentence.

Here are a few examples of compound-complex sentences:

- I needed a new computer, so I got a laptop because they're portable.

- The students were excited; they could go home early because of the power outage.

Identify the Type of Sentence:

Identify whether the following sentences are simple, compound or complex sentences. Also, mention which of the clauses is the main clause and the subordinate clause.

1.   I did not know that this food was meant only for the staff.
2.   She is innocent, so she has appealed to the court.
3.   If you are not ready with the song, it is better to let them know.
4.   She will come home or I will stay back at her place.
5.   In the evening, I am going to the park.
6.   The sun looks amazing today.
7.   I remember the day that we met very well.
8.   Nithi is not keeping well, yet she decided to go to work.
9.   After they reach the hotel, they will inform us.
10.   We are going to the park.

Answers:

1.   I did not know that this food was meant only for the staff.

   Sentence Type – Complex sentence

   Main Clause – I did not know

   Subordinate Clause – That this food was meant only for the staff

2.   She is innocent, so she has appealed to the court.

   Sentence Type – Compound sentence

   Main Clause – She is innocent

   Main Clause – She has appealed to the court

3.   If you are not ready with the song, it is better to let them know.

   Sentence Type – Complex Sentence

   Main Clause – It is better to let them know

   Subordinate Clause – If you are not ready with the song

4. She will come home or I will stay back at her place.

    Sentence Type – Compound Sentence

    Main Clause – She will come home

    Main Clause – I will stay back at her place

5. In the evening, I am going to the park.

    Sentence Type – Simple Sentence

    Main Clause – I am going to the park

6. The sun looks amazing today.

    Sentence Type – Simple Sentence

    Main Clause – The sun looks amazing today

7. I remember the day that we met very well.

    Sentence Type – Complex Sentence

    Main Clause – I remember the day very well

    Subordinate Clause – That we met

8. Nithi is not keeping well, yet she decided to go to work.

    Sentence Type – Compound Sentence

    Main Clause – Nithi is not keeping well

    Main Clause – She decided to go to work

9. After they reach the hotel, they will inform us.

    Sentence Type – Complex Sentence

    Main Clause – They will inform us

    Subordinate Clause – After they reach the hotel

10. We are going to the park.

    Sentence Type – Simple Sentence

    Main Clause – We are going to the park

Source:

https://byjus.com/english/simple-compound-complex-sentences-exercises/
https://www.grammarly.com/

Unit-V
COMMON ENGLISH

5.1. Listening and Speaking

Learning is some kind of internal change and it can be noticed by external change in the learners' behaviour, attitude, interest, abilities and knowledge repertoire. This Unit consists of topics that works towards that change as along with skill development and literary development activities, the skills in using the language are employed.

Among all the skills, listening skill is mostly ignored by many; and they opt to take it for granted. Though listening skill seems to be passive, it is the most needed for effective application of speaking skill. Listening and Speaking are interrelated; and with the sole purpose of initiating creative process in the learners, different aspects of listening and speaking skills are introduced. Opportunities are created for our learners to integrate these skills, so that there is a move from "skill-learning" to "skill-getting" with its impact in "skill-using"; and from "stage of accuracy" to "stage of fluency" with its effect in the "stage of production". Along with grammatical contexts, career and attitude-oriented practice are given through the topics to enhance the learners' employability.

5.1.1. Informal interview for feature writing

Source: https://skillsforchange.com/what-is-a-formal-interview/

Interview is a special word, especially for fresh graduates and those who are awaiting for a job/switching over from one job to another. The expression "interview" refers to a structured conversation between an interviewer and an interviewee; in which questions are asked by the interviewer, and the candidate responds to the questions. This feature is common in all interviews. An interview may also be considered a transfer of information on both directions.

1. Formal vs Informal Interviews

To have a clear understanding, let us see the difference between formal and informal interviews. Interview processes can be categorized into two methods: Formal and Informal interviews.

Traditional interviews, otherwise known as **formal interviews** include interviews for getting a job or applying for a study program. They are conducted in a more formal setting by a panel of people, specifically higher-level executives/individuals with more experience and senior titles as they have more knowledge of the company and its processes. They just observe and evaluate the multiple aspects of the candidates. Many companies follow formal interviews to test the ability of the candidates. The attire chosen by the candidate should also be formal. The selection process includes multiple rounds and it's more systematic. In such employer-oriented interview, fewer personal questions are asked and focus is given more on professional questions.

Source: https://totempool.com/blog/formal-informal-interview/

On the other hand, **informal interviews** are held in a casual setting. They give a wonderful opportunity to share with the employer what the candidate could do to an organization. Without the formalities of an official environment, the communication style as well as personality of the employee is observed by the potential employer. Strict procedures are not followed in informal interviews. Generally, informal interviews are conducted when an employee requests advice, or when he badly needs more information about a specific topic, or to assess whether that candidate fits that company. Similar to traditional interview, the interviewee needs to prepare well for this interview too.

i. **Informal Interview: Is there need for Pre-preparation !**

Informal interviews have the same goals similar to structured interview. But they are conducted outside the office, might be over coffee, brunch, lunch etc. They are also used to assess whether that particular candidate is interested in fitting together with the company. The key phases required to make yourself getting ready for informal interviews are enlisted below:

- Review/Research on the company

- Analysing the requirements of the job

- Appraising your academic eligibility

- Appropriateness of your long-term goals and your suitability to the job

- Balance between formal and casual

Along with this preparation, the learners can also frame questions that is asked by the interviewer by themselves and practice them with their peers. It helps them to know where they need more preparation and in what they are lacking.

ii. Guidelines: Informal interview

Similar to formal interview, the candidate should equip himself/herself with responses to the questions that are asked by the interviewer. A few questions that you can expect in informal interviews are given below:

1. Tell me about yourself (or) Introduce yourself.

2. Why do you choose this profession? Is it your choice?

3. How do you feel about working nights and weekends?

4. What is your formula of success?

Apart from these questions, s/he also should be ready with the questions that s/he needs clarifications from the interviewer. A few questions are enlisted:

1. Can you tell me a little more about why you reached out to me?

2. What are some challenges the company is currently dealing with?

3. What type of training and development opportunities are normally provided?

4. What is the next stage in the recruitment process?

At the end of the interview, ask if there is anything else they need to know, or that you have not covered properly.

Exercise

1. Visualize that you are interviewing your role model to write a feature for your college e-magazine and prepare the questions.

2. Draft a few questions to interview a government hospital doctor to know the impact of Covid pandemic situation on his profession.

3. Formulate questions to interview an engineering college professor to write a feature on the stress management during working hours.

4. Assume you are attending an interview for your dream designation and prepare at least five questions that you would like to ask your interviewer.

5.1.2. Listening and responding to questions at a formal interview

A formal interview is a one-on-one meeting between a prospective job candidate and employer. It has been the norm for decades to select an employee. It is a type of employment test, held in a formal way. This is also called a planned interview.

The candidate is informed about the interview well in advance and the interviewer plans and prepares questions for the interview and the selection of the employee is based on the requirements and procedures of the company. The candidate should also be prepared for questions that will be asked during the job interview. What to say and how to say is very important during the interview. The employee is expected to justify and amplify his/her views in a rational and logical manner. Responses should be supported by statistical data, or additional information. Based on the performance, the employer decides whether the candidate is right or not, for the position.

1. Types of Interviews:

Basically, there are three types of interviews - structured, unstructured, and behavioral. It is not a task to identify whether the interview is structured, unstructured or behavioural. A few tips are provided below -

Structured interview may be rigid and formal. A definite set of questions will be asked to the job applicant. A typical question might be "What are your career goals and objectives?"

Unstructured interview is more informal and more conversational. Some general questions are asked, but there will be more give and take of information. In an extremely unstructured interview, the recruiter may ask very few questions and initiate a discussion of your qualifications. It might open with the statement "Tell me something about yourself / Introduce yourself."

In a **behavioral interview**, the recruiter will ask very pointed questions regarding how you have handled specific kinds of situations especially critical situations, or how you would deal with the kinds of challenges you have experienced in your previous job. A typical question might be "Tell me how you handled a recent conflict situation."

Interviews are also conducted in the following ways:

- Panel Interview - In this type of interview, there are multiple interviewers who assess one candidate

- Group Interview – In this interview, multiple applicants are interviewed at the same time. It is challenging for the candidates; and it can be challenging for the interviewing panel as well.

- Phone (or) Pre-screen Interview - Hiring managers often suggest a phone call as a first stage interview

- Video Interview – It is like a face-to-face interview. But the interviewer or a panel of interviewers ask you questions online on a service like Skype. Microsoft Teams etc.

- Lunch Interview / Off-site Interview - The point of the meal interview is - to know each other well (you and employer), and to observe how you conduct yourself in a social setting. It is customary for the employer to pay for the meal. But this is not limited to entry level job test.

- Task Interview- It is the instructional tests that you complete as part of a job interview

- Case Interview – It is a hypothetical business situation that is presented during an interview process to determine how a candidate thinks about a particular critical situation

- Stress Interview – It is a technique used to put applicants under immense tension and your response and decision making will be tested.

- Whatever be the style of interview, it's very important to be prepared, self-confident and flexible. Remember that interview is the only way to demonstrate the fact that the candidate possesses the appropriate skills. Good preparation and planning are keys to success in interviews (https://hrmpractice.com/what-is-a-formal-interview-2/).

2. Facts to be Noted before attending Interview

- Write down the location, time and name of the interviewer with his contact number. Make sure to reach the location of interview spot earlier.

- Go through the website and research on the details of the organization, especially achievements, annual reports, brochures, newsletters etc.

- If possible, make use of the career service available in the website and practice interviews for challenging questions.

- Familiarize with your resume/curriculum vitae, application form and covering letter.

- It's a good idea to bring a resume to a formal interview, even if the employer already has a copy.

- If there's need to think and respond during the interview, say politely, 'that's a very interesting question, I would like a moment to think about that', or ask the question to be repeated.

- Elude from criticizing former employers or colleagues as it creates bad impression.

- Avoid interrupting or arguing with the interviewer.

Apart from this preparation, a candidate for a formal interview should dress appropriately as it proclaims his/her character. It creates a good impression and adds to the better performance at the interview (**https://www.moravian.edu › basic-interview-formats**).

3. Interview Questions

Exercise

Read the Interview questions given below carefully. Prepare answers for all the questions using the clues given in brackets. Let your answers be meaningful, effective and genuine.

A sample answer for the first question is given. Similar to this, you can prepare your own answers based on your interest, skills, abilities and qualifications.

1. **Tell me about yourself/Introduce yourself:**

    [Clue: The interviewer is trying to find out about you, your job skills and how well you express yourself. Do not dwell on personal matters including your family details unless it's asked. State your best qualifications for the job. Be specific. Try to show that you meet the employer's expectations.]

    Some samples are given below for your reference. Go through each one and prepare a self-introduction in your own words highlighting your abilities and skills.

SAMPLE 1: Introduce yourself briefly.

Good morning Sir.

I am Seenu Natarajan **from** Madurai.

I completed my PG and UG Micro-biology in GT College, Madurai.

I did my schooling in T.V.S. Hr. Sec. School, Madurai.

My hobbies are drawing, painting and listening music.

My aim is to do a good job in Micro-biology industry and I would like to help my country to develop economically.

Thank you sir.

SAMPLE 2 : Tell me about yourself and your family.

Good morning Sir.

It's my pleasure to introduce myself.

I am Albert Suresh. **My native is** Chennai. **I am a fresher.**

About my qualification:

I have completed my M.A., English with an aggregate of 75% in 2022. I did my schooling with 86% in 12th standard and 75% in 10th standard in N M V Higher Secondary School, Salem.

My technical skills are C, C++, HTML and XML.

About my family,

My family consists of 4 members including me, my father - a Business man, my mother – a Dentist and my elder brother - a worker in Sutherland Global Service.

Coming to my hobbies,

My hobbies are like playing table tennis, making new friends, watching movies a lot and listening to songs. I have done some short films too.

To say about my Work Experience,

I worked as a Part-Time Educational consultant in a Consultancy when I was doing my under graduation (UG).

My greatest strength is I don't give up easily. I am cool, calm and very friendly. I am very broad minded and hardworking too. I'm also a quick learner.

My weakness is my laziness, and believing others easily.

I never feel comfortable until I finish my work in time.

About my **professional interest**:

My short-term goal is to complete my degree and to get a good job in a famous company like yours, where I can upgrade my skills and knowledge efficiently.

My long-term goal is to reach a respectable position in a company where I am working, in which they never want to lose me at any cost.

Regarding languages

I know English and Tamil very well. I can read Hindi.

Thank you sir.

2. **What are your long-term goals or career plans?**

   [Clue: The interviewer may want to know about your career goals. The interviewer may also want to know what expectation you have of the company.]

3. **a) What do you feel are your greatest strengths?**

   [Clue: This is your opportunity to brag a little bit. It is important that you have done your research about the type of work that you are applying for. For example, if you are applying for the post of a production labourer; and from your research you understand that the particular type of work required people that have the ability to meet quotas, work as a team and make improvement suggestions, then it is important for you to incorporate this into your strengths.]

   b) What do you feel are your weaknesses?

   [Clue: You never want to give any indication of any weaknesses that you have. Turn your weaknesses into strengths by working it to the employer's advantage.]

4. **Why do you want to work for this company? Why are you interested in this job?**

   [Clue: The interviewer is trying to determine what you know about the company, and whether you will be willing to make a commitment to the job. If your skills match the job requirements, say as many positive things about the company as possible, show your interest in whatever products they sell; or whatever services they do and explain why the position fits with your career goals.]

5. What kind of training or qualifications do you have?

[Clue: The interviewer is trying to find out what school/college/ university credentials you have. If you have no formal educational qualifications, then say about your work experience.]

6. What do you do in your spare time?

[Clue: Interviewers ask this question to see if your activities and hobbies might help the company; and to get an idea of what kind of person you are outside your work life. Describe any volunteer work you do and any hobbies or interests that might relate to the job in some way. Stick to active hobbies, such as reading books, playing sports, carpentry, gardening, etc. Avoid mentioning inactive and non-creative activities such as watching television.]

7. How do you react to instruction and criticism?

[Clue: The interviewer is trying to find out how you get along with supervisors and how you feel about authority.]

8. How well do you work under pressure or tight deadlines?

[Clue: This question indicates that the job you're applying for will involve working under pressure. Give examples of volunteer and paid work that involved pressure and deadlines.]

9. What five words would be describing you?

[Clue: These should be your transferrable skills such as reliable, punctual, organized, friendly, honest, cooperative, outgoing, easy to get along with, hardworking, energetic, take pride in my work, responsible, respected, and dedicated.]

10. What type of salary are you looking for?

[Clue: Do not get into this subject unless you are asked. Even then, you want to leave an impression that you are flexible in this area.]

5.2. Reading and Writing

Reading is an active process. It helps the readers to interact with the text and construct meaning in the process of understanding the content. In real life, we are driven by the desire to read either for pleasure or for getting information. The varied kinds of reading such as skimming, scanning, intensive reading, extensive reading etc. enhance the reader's speed of reading as well as the level of comprehension and make them mastering the mechanics of reading. Motivating the readers to write is a challenging task for the language teacher. But reading practice leads to the integration of skills; and it also facilitates writing (PGCTE Course Material). This topic initiates interests in the learners as it's on applying for their dream jobs, preparing skits, and readers' theatre which makes them write in their own style and format.

5.2.1. Writing letters of application

Letter writing is a skill. It is both an art and a technique. Of all the forms of writing, letter writing can be considered the most challenging and rewarding (R.P.Bhatnagar, 2009). Today's computer age has superfast methods of communication such as e-mail, fax etc.

Letters can be categorized under two headings- **Informal and Formal.**

Informal Letters - Personal Letters including letters to parents, friends, relatives etc. fall under this category.

Formal Letters - Formal letters can be grouped and sorted as given below - Business Letters, Official letters and Job Application / Resume with Covering Letter.

In this text, let us have a detailed outlook on the format, form and elements of job applications as well as Covering Letter. It's time to start your practice.

1. **A Few Guidelines for a Better Presentation of RESUME**

The term 'RESUME' is used in the United States. Its equivalent 'CURRICULUM VITAE' (CV) is preferred in England and European Countries. It is also used in India but of late "RESUME" has gained higher frequency of use.

Resume writing is the first step in securing a job. It is a marketing tool for obtaining an interview, not a job. You may have excellent subject knowledge and wonderful skill and talent. But unless you communicate them explicitly, you may not be able to reach the interview stage.

In the modern context, a resume should be considered a standalone document that a candidate submits to a potential employer expressing his/her interest in an open position. It is the content of the resume that determines whether or not you should be called for an interview. It is also your first indirect contact with your employer. The employers receive hundreds / thousands of resumes every day. If they look the same, it will be dull and dreary. So, take care that your resume should have clarity, brevity, accuracy and courtesy which makes it different from that of others in all respects (R.P.Bhatnagar, 2009).

2. **Types of Resume**

There are three types of Resumes: Chronological Resume, Functional Resume and Combination Resume.

(https://resumegenius.com/resume-samples/human-resources-hr-resume-example)

Chronological Resume requires the details of educational qualification mentioned from Under graduate to post graduation and other further qualifications in the chronological Order.

Functional Resume focuses more on highlighting the strong features of the resume in terms of educational qualification/

technical as well as soft skills acquired and mastered, and various other additional achievements/accomplishments. This type is presently more popular as it showcases the applicant's positive, job-specific qualification.

Combination Resume draws from the best of both types. It gives information about the applicant's history of education in a chronological manner while also highlighting the strong features of the applicant's many skills and internship experiences that reinforce the aptness of the applicant as a suitable candidate for the job.

3.   **Main Purpose of the Resume**

Resume can be prepared in the format which suits your job needs. Whatever type it be, a resume can be considered a marketing tool; and the main purpose of the resume is to sell yourself.

Hence - Find out what type of candidates, the employer has in his mind and you should design your resume accordingly. Find out whether your qualifications, experience, talents and personal skills match with the employment needs and job requirement. The next step is to do a SWOT [strengths – weakness – opportunities – threats] analysis. Outline your skills, abilities, work experience and extracurricular activities. What are your strong features and what makes you unique? Make sure you convey this information in your resume.

The following four items of information given below form the 'nuts and bolts' of your resume:

EMPLOYER'S / EMPLOYMENT NEEDS	EMPLOYEE'S RESUME CONTENT
• What are you? • What have you done so far? • What can you do for us? • What are your further plans?	• Your education, experience and personal skills • Your past professional accomplishments • Your plan for the development of the organization • Your professional growth and its contribution to the organization

So, start designing your resume that could be your ticket to the job of your dreams. Let your resume speak for you even before you enter the interview hall. Always make a rough resume with all the details before you finalize onto the fair one.

4. Formatting your Resume

Here are some tips to help you in formatting your resume.

- Keep the font size within 10 - 12.

- Use A4 sheet and a skilled looking font such as Times New Roman, Ariel or Helvetica.

- Avoid italics, script and underlined words.

- Use non-decorative typefaces. Choose one typeface and stick to it.

- Do not fold your resume. If there's need to mail your resume, put it in a large envelope.

- Resume is for freshers. So, limit the length of your resume up to 2 pages.

- Curriculum Vitae (CV) is for experienced candidates. So, it can be formatted up to 4 or 5 pages.

- It is advisable to use bulleted sentence format as it makes reading easier. Bulleted sentences that begin with action words like 'Prepared', 'Monitored', and 'Presented' are more impressive.

- Proofread and be sure to catch all spelling errors, grammatical weaknesses, unusual punctuation and inconsistent capitalizations.

- Laser print it on plain/white paper.

i. Build your Resume

There is no standard format for preparing your resume. But a resume should summarize your education, skills, accomplishments and experiences. We can go through the basic categories, which help you to draft a resume.

1. NAME, ADDRESS AND TELEPHONE:

You have to give your permanent address with e-mail address, phone number in the left corner. For example,

SANJAY AMULRAJ

42, Geetanjali apartment

Kodambakkam High Road

Chennai – 16

Mobile: 98462 38576

E mail : sanjay.r@yahoo.com

Affix your recent
passport size
photo if asked

2. OBJECTIVE:

It should be brief and to the point. It must give the employer an idea about your work preferences and where you want to be in your career in future. For example:

Seeking a challenging position with opportunities for career advancement and learning.

or

To have a long career in the particular field (mention your field of interest here), gain further skills and attain the goal of the organization aiming at mutual growth.

3. EDUCATION:

Here, include your degree, specialization, institutions attended, year of graduation, subsidiary subjects studied, and any related courses or projects done. You can give your qualifications separately as professional [PG/ Engineering/Research], academic [UG/+2/S.S.L.C.] and technical [Computer skills, typing, shorthand ...]. Educational qualifications should be presented in the reverse order. Your highest educational qualification should top the list of your academic record. For example:

i.   PROFESSIONAL QUALIFICATION:

- M.C.A.: First Class with distinction – 88% May 2022

  PSG College of Engineering & Technology

  Coimbatore.

ii.   ACADEMIC QUALIFICATION:

- B.C.A.: First Class with distinction – 86% May, 2020

  St. Xavier's College of Arts and Science

  42, Church Gate Road

  Mumbai – 400 001.

- Standard XII: Computer Science: First Class – 80% May 2017

  St.Xavier's Hr. Sec. School,

  Mumbai.

- S.S.L.C.: First class – 88% May 2015

  St.Xavier's High School,

  Mumbai.

  You can also use tabular column for this educational entry.

iii. TECHNICAL SKILLS:

- Computer Literacy: C, C++, Advanced java, Oracle
- Good knowledge on Internet Security
- E-Commerce transactions
- System Analysis and any other technical skills you possess.

4. RESEARCH PUBLICATIONS:

In the current scenario, if you apply for teaching post in Colleges/ Universities, research publications play a vital role. So, include your publication details, projects and patents if you have any. For example,

- *The Stratagem for Efficiency in Communiqué.* International Journal of Research and Analytical Reviews (IJRAR). Impact Factor 5.75. UGC approved Journal Number 43602. Vol. 7, Issue 2, June 2020. E-ISSN 2348-1269, P- ISSN 2349-5138. 56-62.

  If you apply for any other job where there is no need for publications, you can avoid it.

5. CO-CURRICULAR ACTIVITIES:

Here, mention the projects done by you in your UG/PG. For example:

PROJECT 1 (MCA)

Title: Poll Designer and its Impact

Duration: 5 months

Software Requirements: Visual Studio.Net, SQL Server 2000 / MSAccess

Description:

Poll Designer is a powerful .NET web control that will let you create any poll in seconds. It is very easy to use and is composed of two key controls. The poll box web control shows all answers of your poll in the specified format. This control can be used directly with the VS.NET visual designer or web matrix, however real questions / answers of your poll will only show up on a page served by IIS.

PROJECT 2 (BCA):

Title   :

Team Size   :

Language   :

Software   :

Objective   :

6. **EXTRA CURRICULAR ACTIVITIES:**

Activities regarding Sports, Games etc. come under this category. For example:

- Won State level Trophy in Football conducted in Thiyagaraja College, Madurai, 20 November 2021.

7. **SKILL SUMMARY / SKILL SETS:**

Here include your skills such as:

- Positive attitude

- Problem solving skill

- Individual as well as Team work

- Fluent in Tamil, English and Hindi

8. **WORK EXPERIENCE / CAREER GRAPH / EMPLOYMENT HISTORY:**

Here you should give the details regarding the place you have worked, the position you held, your responsibilities and achievements (projects done, targets achieved), the dates or period you have served in the organization etc... Use action words to describe your job duties. The work experience should begin with your present position and move back to the entry level appointment. Include the following information: Title of position, Name of Organization, Location of work (town, state), Dates of employment and Description of your work responsibilities with emphasis on achievements.

For example:

1.   June 2020 – till date: K.H.TEHNICAL SUPPORT INC, Sipcot, Ranipet

Sales Manager – Senior

- Establish corporate accounting systems and procedures with the design of a computerized system for current accounting practices.

9.   PERSONAL PROFILE or PERSONAL DATA:

Your personal details like - your name, father's name, date of birth, permanent address and contact number, e-mail, passport details, hobbies, languages known etc... should be given here. While writing 'Languages Known', you have to mention whether you can "Read / Speak / Write'. For example

Languages Known:

- Tamil   : Read / Speak / Write

- English : Read / Speak / Write

- Hindi   : Speak

There is absolutely no need to write about your family background, marital status and health. Even hobbies like stamp and coin collecting are considered outdated.

10. REFERENCES:

The resume generally has reference as last detail. It is the usual practice to cite three persons – two to certify your professional skills, managerial abilities and academic records; and the third one to support your character and family background. Fresh candidates can cite their professors, research guides and department heads. References should be given with prior consent from the relevant people. This must include their name, posting, address and phone number. It is not essential to give reference in a resume. You can state that-

References: References can be furnished if needed.

or

References furnished on request.

11. DECLARATION:

A resume should end with Declaration. The usual format is-

I hereby declare that the above given details are true to my knowledge and belief. If given chance, I would do my duty sincerely and honestly.

Thanking you

Place: Yours sincerely,

Date   S/d

                                                      [Your Name]

ii. Electronic Resume

Most of the companies have their own web page where they upload their application form with details of job requirements. You can download the relevant form and fill in and send it by post or even transmit it on line. The internet-based resume has certain distinct features. It is the computer that sorts out the electronic resumes. The computer is programmed to read keywords like nouns or short phrases rather than action words. If the computer evaluates that, there is a match between job requirements and your skills, talents and education highlighted by keywords, you are sure to be selected for interview. Repetition of keywords may not help you in any way. Visual appeal like different fonts, italics, bold face, underlining etc.. may have no effect on the computer and they are not required in an electronic resume.

iii. Covering Letter

Formal letter writing should be followed in the preparation of a covering letter. A rightly formatted letter has three parts namely Salutation, Body of the letter and a Complimentary Close.

* **Salutation**- A formal way of addressing the person, to whom the letter is written. (Eg.)

Dear Sir, (or) Dear Madam, (or) Dear Sir/Madam,

After the Salutation, mention the 'Subject' of your application. If there is any previous correspondence, type it in 'Reference' with date.

- Subject   : Application for the post of _______________

- Reference: (if needed)

- **Body of the letter:**

Introduce your purpose of the letter. Mention your qualification with reference to your academic achievements and other additional skills acquired by you with certification. You can also give your various other extra accomplishments that you find relevant for this job position.

Convery thanks for the opportunity to apply and assure your best in the event of being selected for the job.

- **Complimentary Close -**

Leave two lines of space after your last paragraph. Then use a conventional closing.

Eg. Yours sincerely, /Yours respectfully, /Yours truly,

Four lines after the closing, type your full name. Put your signature in between.

Eg.   Yours sincerely

[Dr.RADHA MATHIVANAN]

Sample Covering Letter:

SANJAY AMULRAJ

42, Geetanjali apartment

Kodambakkam High Road

Chennai – 16

Email ID : **sanjay.r@yahoo.com**

Mobile   : 98462 38576

Dear Hiring Manager,

Subject : Application for the post of Professor/English

I am writing to apply for the position of Professor currently offered at Clearwater University. Teaching has been my lifelong career, and I am excited to reach new heights in the field of education. As a dedicated researcher with a passion for knowledge and learning.

Previously, I was employed at St. Helena University, and there I competently taught UG classes of 40 students. I also offered personalized tutoring services to many of them during office hours. In both student and peer reviews, I was consistently commended for being easy to understand, good in assisting the students in working through problems.

Both as an educator and student, my attention to detail has always been one of my strong points. As a professional, I feel it is my duty to ensure everything I do is done correctly and to the highest degree of excellence - whether that is grading papers, reviewing lesson plans or collaborating with my peers to establish academic goals for the department.

Thank you for your time and consideration of my application. Herewith I attach my Resume for your kind reference.

Yours sincerely

Sanjay Amulraj

Prepare your Covering Letter and then attach your Resume after it; and then mail/post it as per the requirement.

(For samples, visit **https://novoresume.com/career-blog/cover-letter-examples** and **https://www.indeed.com/career-advice/cover-letter-samples)**

Exercise

1. Draft an application to the Principal of an Arts and Science College, applying for the post of an Assistant Professor in your discipline.

2. Prepare a job application to the Editor of a famous newspaper for the post of a Reporter (at the National level)

3. Design your Resume in your own words highlighting your skills. Attach a covering letter.

5.2.2. Readers' Theatre

Just like different discourses in writing, there are different ways of reading too. Of course, all are familiar with reading different genres in literature, especially a short story, poem, one act play etc. This section inspires and initiates the learners to know how to write and perform in scripts. Indeed, plays and dramas require a highly stylized version of reading. When a student performs before the audience, his/her role is to be spoken with a lot of intensity, intonation changes and in a loud voice. It also needs a good grasp of the language, specifically how to speak using an understandable accent and with proper punctuation and pronunciation. Let's move on to Readers' Theatre.

Readers' Theatre is a particular type of dramatic pedagogy, which shares literature and uses scripts and performance to enhance the comprehension of a text. It is a strategy for developing reading fluency. It initiates reading aloud activity as the learners have to enact their role in scripts. It also makes the learners work collaboratively.

1. **Readers' Theatre: Why?**

    - It promotes fluency.

    - It helps readers learn to read aloud with expression.

    - It helps build reading confidence.

2. **How to use Readers' Theatre?**

- Choose a story that can be divided into parts, or character.

- Assign reading parts to each one.

- Ask students to read their scripts orally for practice.

- Make them read assigned parts to the audience.

3. **The features of a Reader's Theatre**

- Improves fluency through fun learning

- Practice collaborative learning skills

- Develops listening and speaking skills

4. **Points to be Noted**

- The beauty of the Readers' Theatre lies in the scripts. Some students and a positive attitude are needed for effective performance. There's no need for props, a set, and costumes.

- Nametags and headband with the character's name can be used for understanding the concept and the story. But it's not necessary.

- The goal of Readers' Theatre is not memorization but to practice reading fluency, and not to create a performance.

As the target is fluency in reading with modulation in voice, the students should read through the script atleast 3 times – First Read, Practice Read and Performance Read. This practice helps them to develop confidence in reading English fearlessly and it establishes good audience etiquette. In excitement, the students automatically gets involved in the performance.

(https://www.scriptreaderpro.com/drama-script-examples/)

Exercise 1 (for writing)

The class can be divided into groups of five (one teacher and four students) and read the short story entitled "Lamb to the Slaughter" (written by Roald Dahl) by clicking the link given below. The team should prepare the play in brief, without changing the flow of the story and the suspense should be maintained.

https://docs.google.com/document/edit?id=1kSb-ORZvVJIEe3ty DnpYxjPuJ4_LVpwzvnp_VXtIaOw&hl=en&pli=1

Questions for Discussion:

1. "Please," she begged. "Please eat it. Personally, I couldn't touch a thing, certainly not what's been in the house when he was here. But it's all right for you. It'd be a favor to me if you'd eat it up. Then you can go on with your work again afterwards."

   Who said this to whom? What does she want them to eat? What work are they engaged in?

Exercise 2 (for performance)

1. The class can be divided into groups of five (one teacher and four students) and made to play the short play entitled "Decomposition" by clicking the link given below and reading aloud. The teacher can help in the intonation and presentation of the text.

   The concluding part can be done by the students themselves. They can create their own concluding part.

    https://www.studocu.com/ph/document/xavier-university-ateneo-de-cagayan/senior-high-school/decomposition-a-very-short-play-script-sample/20485219

5.2.3. Dramatizing everyday situations/social issues through skits Writing Scripts and Performing

1. **What is a Skit?**

   A skit is a short parody in which performers mock different aspects of life, whether that be a person, situation or an existing piece of literature, film, or television. They are usually satirical in their writing and presentation (https://blog.celtx.com/how-to-write-a-skit/). They are also sometimes referred to as sketches. A skit should be original with a clear idea. Reading comic stories or watching humorous videos might initiate or inspire one to prepare the skit. A skit writer should have funny ideas and sense of humour as an exciting skit show will always be captivating to watch. But it should not be too lengthy.

2. **Features of the Skit**

- Determine the genre and length of your skit.

- Decide what you are attempting to do with your story. Do you wish to convey a message or just make your audience laugh? What tone would you like to set?

- To make a skit, start by thinking of ideas that make you laugh.

- Write down interesting thoughts related to that idea. Then develop it.

- Outline the developed idea.

- Even if the skit is small, it should have a beginning, middle and an end. The introduction can be normal everyday situation; the middle part should express out of the normal or out-of-box thinking. The final part i.e. climax should have resolution.

- Prepare rough draft first.

- Write the title of the skit. Then give the characters involved in that scene.

- Parenthesis can be used to mention actions.

- Start your skit, build the action up, keep improving your draft by removing unnecessary dialogues and actions.

- Write out final draft of your scene, rehearse, and finally perform your skit. If possible, you can upload your skit in YouTube channels for watching. **(https://proessaywriter.net)**

Skits are a powerful medium of communicating the emerging social problems. Skits are a part of students' curriculum as well. They learn course content from skits in classrooms. They also learn about themselves and each other through skits. Relationships in college can be challenging and skits are an excellent way to help college students deal with relationship problems.

Through skits and role plays, they learn to express their views and they develop their communication skills, presentation skills etc. Skits on various social sensitive issues like dowry, corruption, gender discrimination etc. are being organized by students' time to time (https://www.iudehradun.edu.in).

A Sample Skit: Not Enough Parachutes

Characters: Pilot, President, Camper, Smartest man in the world

Preparation:

Line up 4 chairs in a column sideways to the audience. These chairs serve as seats on the plane. The campers should sit in the following order: the camper at the back, then the smart man, and the President. The Pilot stands by the plane.

Pilot: (to arriving passengers) "Good afternoon. Please tell me who you are, so I can check our passenger list."

President (quite importantly): "I am the President of the United States."

Pilot: "Welcome aboard, Mr. President. Please take a seat."

The Pilot repeats this for each passenger and they respond as follows:

Smart Man (very importantly): "I am the Smartest Man in the World. I've just been awarded this wonderful 'Smart Guy' award and I am heading to my office to think about important things."

Camper: "I am a Camper on my way to summer camp." (Or make up something specific for your group.)

Pilot (after each passenger makes their response): "Welcome aboard. Please take a seat."

Pilot (taking his seat): "This is your pilot. We are cleared for take-off. Please buckle your seatbelts and enjoy the ride."

The plane takes off and everyone looks out the windows for a few seconds.

Pilot looks nervously at controls, taps instruments, and then addresses passengers: "I'm sorry to report that we have a major malfunction. The plane is losing altitude and we will crash in just a few minutes. We will need to parachute to safety. Please follow me."

The Pilot gets up and walks to the rear of plane with the President, Smartest Man, and camper falling in line behind him.

The Pilot counts parachutes and addresses passengers: "I have more bad news. We only have 3 parachutes."

President (pushing past pilot and grabbing a parachute): "I am the President! My country needs me!" He jumps out.

Smart Man (pushing past pilot and grabbing a parachute) "I am the world's Smartest Man! I must live so I can do important things!" He jumps out.

Pilot (to camper): "Well, there's only one chute left. You take it. I guess the pilot will go down with his ship."

Camper: "Actually, there are 2 parachutes left."

Pilot: "Really? How is that possible?"

Camper: "Well, the Smartest Man in the World just jumped out with my knapsack!" (https://icebreakerideas.com)

Exercise

The class can be divided into groups (as per the story requires); and each group can write a short skit on a social issue of their choice and enact it before the class.

5.3. WORD POWER

5.3.1. COLLOCATION

1. Definition

Collocation is 'a predictable combination of words'; it is a familiar grouping of words which often goes together because of their habitual use. It's inseparable. For example, when it rains heavily, we tend to say 'big rain' instead of 'heavy rain'. Though it conveys the same meaning, it sounds strange. Example:

- *to do homework*

- *to make the bed*

i. Common mistakes with collocations

1. I very enjoyed the party. - incorrect

✓ I really enjoyed the party. - correct

2. I've made my homework. - incorrect

✓ I've done my homework. - correct

3. I had a strong meal this morning. - incorrect

✓ I had a heavy meal this morning. - correct

4. I lost the train so I was late. - incorrect

✓ I missed the train so I was late. - correct

5. I did a mistake. - incorrect

✓ I made a mistake. - correct

ii. Characteristics of Collocation

- Follows a particular order

- Helps in adhering to proper structure of the English language

- Helps in beautifying the language

- Makes the language natural and interesting

- Enhances the use of language and thereby comparatively leads to innovation of the English language

iii. Patterns in Collocation

Collocation can be made from combinations of varied parts of speech - noun, verb, adjective, adverb etc. The main types of collocations are: noun + noun, noun + verb, noun + preposition, verb + noun, verb + prepositional phrase, verb + adverb, adjective + noun, adjective + preposition, adjective + adverb, adverb + adjective, adverb + preposition and adverb + adverb. There are a lot of collocations in the above-mentioned patterns. Some examples are given below -

1. Noun collocations:

In this type of collocations, a noun / a verb / a preposition can be used with a noun to form the group of words.

i. Noun + Noun Collocation

Example:

- *Forensic science is a **growth industry**.*
- *This road is closed to **motor vehicles**.*
- *His father signed his **report card**.*

ii. Noun + Verb Collocation

Example:

- *The **economy boomed** in 2002.*
- *The **company has grown** and now employs over 300 people.*
- *The **company has expanded** and now has branches in most major countries.*

iii. Noun + Preposition Collocation

Example:

- *What's the **reason for your unhappiness?**.*
- *He took a **photograph of the mountains**.*

- I like to do a **course in computer programming**.

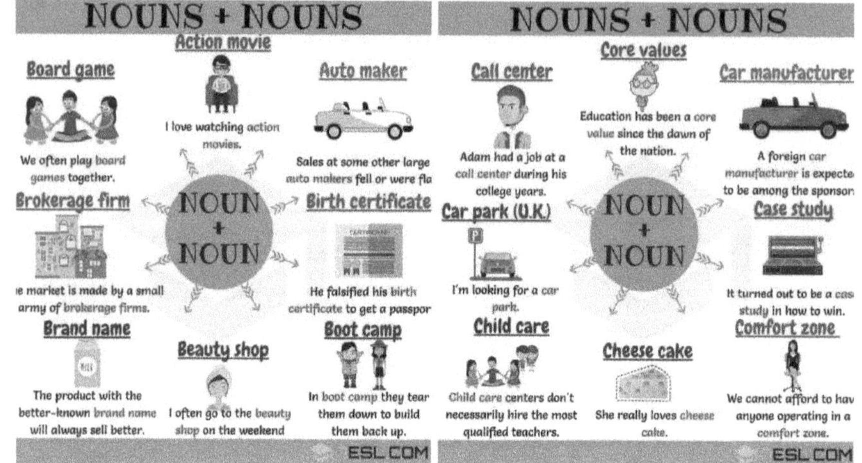

2. Verb Collocations

Collocations which are used commonly tend to involve verb + noun / preposition / adverb formation in the day-to-day situations.

To understand them better, some examples are given below. In each example, the verb has other meaning also.

- To save time

  [A lot of time will be saved if one's concentration is on achieving the target rather than browsing unnecessary topics through the internet.]

- To find a replacement

  [Indian team needs to find a replacement for Sachin as soon as possible.]

i) Verb + Noun Collocation

Example:

- • The internet has **created opportunities** for his company.

- I like to sit down and **do the crossword**.

- Why should I **say sorry** when it's not my fault?

ii.   Verb + Preposition Collocation

Verb + Preposition is also used in our routine life.

For example: made of, give up, throw out, care for, recover from, provide with ......

- The table is ***made of*** teak wood.

- *I **congratulate** you **on** your new job!*

- *John **succeeded in** getting a new job.*

iii)   Verb + Adverb Collocation

Example:

- *He **pulled steadily** on the rope and helped her to safety.*

- *She **placed** the beautiful jar **gently** on the window ledge.*

- *The dedication of the medical staff during the pandemic are **admired greatly.***

3. Adjective Collocations

Adjective Collocations can be formed with noun / preposition / adverb. Listed below a few examples:

i.   Adjective + Noun Collocation

Example:

- *Unemployment is a **major problem** for the government these days.*

- *Women demanded **equal rights**.*

- *It's a cold **rainy day** in October.*

ii.   Adjective + Preposition Collocation

Example:

- *The town is **famous for** its cheese.*

- *I'm quite **good at** English but I'm **bad at** maths.*

- *They were **successful in** winning the contract.*

iii.   Adjective + Adverb Collocation

Example:

- He was ***affected deeply.***
- They are ***married happily.***
- He was ***injured seriously.***

4. Adverb Collocations

i.   Adverb + Adjective Collocation

Here some common adverb + adjective collocations are enlisted.

- Sam was ***bitterly disappointed*** with the result.
- Snow at this time of the year is ***highly unusual.***
- Information is ***readily available*** for visitors.

ii.   Adverb + Verb Collocation

Example:

- It's a change I ***strongly support.***
- The building was ***badly damaged.***
- I ***never knew*** this truth earlier.

iii.   Adverb + Adverb Collocations

Example:

- He was afraid because he was ***all alone.***
- I can't talk to you ***right now*** as I am busy.
- She knows everything ***pretty well.***

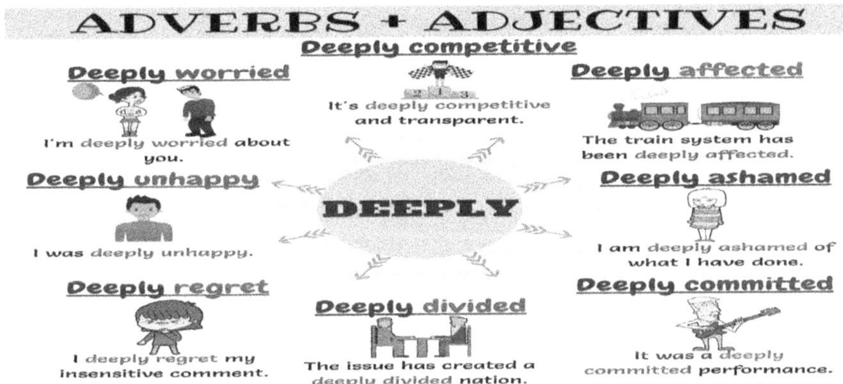

4. Business Collocations

Apart from grammatical contexts, the use of collocations is critical in various types of businesses and work situations. Here, there are numerous ways in which a collocation is formed using verbs, nouns, adjectives, and adverbs. They can be combined with keywords and a business expression can be formed. Some of the important business collocations are:

- Annual *turnover*
- *Break off negotiations*
- *Cease trading*
- *Close a deal*
- *Go bankrupt*
- *Launch a new product*
- *Lay off staff*
- *Take on staff*
- *Counterfeit money*

5. Time Collocations

Common Collocations about Time are enlisted below:

- *Dead on time*
- *From dawn till dusk*
- *Make time for*
- *Great deal of time*
- *Past few weeks*
- *Right on time*
- *Run out of time*
- *Save time*
- *Take your time*
- *Time goes by*

6. Strong, Weak and Fixed Collocations

i. Strong Collocations

Strong collocations are perfect combinations of words that always go together; such as combinations with 'make' and 'do': They sound correct. Such correct usage shows an excellent command of the English language. They usually do not match with many other words.

For example,

- ***Turn on the light.***

- You ***make a cup of tea.***

ii. Weak Collocations

Weak collocations are just the reverse of this strong collocations. The common expression "very interesting" is a weak collocation; but "extremely interesting", and "really interesting" are acceptable substitutes.

For example,

- The expressions "***start a light***" and "***activate a light***" are weak collocations.

- "You ***make your homework***" is also a weak collocation.

iii. Fixed Collocations

Fixed collocations are so strong that they cannot be changed in any way.

For example,

- I ***was walking to and fro***.

The sentence means - I was walking in one direction and then in the opposite direction, a repeated number of times. No other words can replace *to* or *fro* in this collocation. It is completely fixed. These collocations are called idioms.

7. Some commonly used collocations

High earnings	Big earnings
Long-range planning	Long-time planning
Strong coffee	Heavy coffee
Heavy traffic	Large traffic
Happily married	Gladly married
Prices fall	Prices descend
Put on clothes	Wear on clothes
Make a coffee	Do a coffee
Comments on the work	Comments about the work
Choose wisely	Choose smartly

8. Collocations: Collections

Dictionaries such as the Oxford Dictionary of Collocations can help you learn these common collocations. The given weblinks also provide you with a collection of collocations that can be used in daily life.

https://www.englishclub.com/vocabulary/collocations-common.htm

https://vocabularypoint.com/common-collocations-in-english/

A few commonly used collocations are given below.

1. answer the door - open the door after someone knocks the door.

2. arrive on time - to arrive exactly when expected or scheduled to

3. bad temper - a tendency to become angry quickly and easily

4. break news - to tell someone bad news

5. call attention to - to make someone notice or consider someone or something

6. cut costs - to reduce costs

7. deafening silence - a silence that everyone notices

8.   ethical standards - ethically acceptable levels of behaviour

9.   fight a fire - to try to put out a fire

10.   get going – start moving / depart

11.   get rid of - to stop, or remove, something or someone that's annoying

12.   hardly ever - almost never

13.   keep a promise - to do what you promised to do

14.   lay the groundwork - to do preliminary work in preparation for future work

15.   make a fortune - to make a huge amount of money

16.   nervous wreck - a person who's very stressed or nervous

17.   null and void - having no legal effect or force

18.   owe an apology - If you think you owe somebody an apology

19.   pose a threat - create the threat of danger or harm

20.   put out a fire - to stop a fire from burning

21.   room for improvement - the possibility or need for something to improve

22.   run the risk of - to do something risky, or that could have a bad result

23.   stay put - to stay in the same place or situation

24.   travel light - to travel without much luggage

25.   U-turn - a sudden and complete change of policy

26.   vital role - a very important role

27.   wear and tear - damage caused by normal use over time

28.   x-ray vision - the ability to see through objects made of non-transparent materials

29.   yield results - to produce or provide results

30.   zero tolerance - absolutely no tolerance for something

Exercise 1:

Choose the right collocation.

1. We should _________ ready now if we want to be there on time.

    get   have   take   come

2. __________ free to sit wherever you like.

    have   feel   take   come

3. Take the map so that we don't _________ lost.

    feel   get   take   come

4. I didn't win the game, but I ___________ close.

    came   had   took   made

5. Be careful with your cigarette. You don't want your shirt to __________ fire.

    keep   make   catch   do

6. Do try and ____ attention while I'm talking.

    make   do   take   pay

7. We really need to do something to ____ money. I'm broke.

    come   catch   do   make

8. I don't ____ a great relationship with my brother.

    have   come   feel   make

Exercise 2:

Are you ready to see how well you learned collocations? Take a quiz:

1. I have _________ respect for people who work and attend college full-time. It's not easy; you need a lot of dedication!

    Big   great   large

2. There's ___________ evidence that the governor was involved in some illegal activities.

    great   heavy   strong

3. Practicing listening to English every day has resulted in a ___________ improvement in my understanding.

    big   deep   heavy

4. They're expecting ___________ snow this week - classes might be cancelled.

    deep   heavy   strong

5. A ___________ number of our employees have post-graduate degrees.

    big   heavy   large

6. The orchestra made a number of ___________ mistakes in the first performance.

    big   great   strong

7. If you break that iPad you borrowed, you're in ___________ trouble!

    deep   heavy   large

8. Our company has a ___________ commitment to providing the best possible service to our customers.

    heavy   large   strong

9. She received a soccer scholarship due to her ___________ skill on the field.

    big   deep   great

10. My father was a ___________ smoker for many years.

    great   heavy   strong

5.4. Grammar in Context

5.4.1. Working with Clauses

1. What is a Clause?

Phrase and Clause are a part of a sentence but they are different from each other. To understand the function of clauses, the meaning of phrases is also to be learnt.

A Phrase is a group of two or more words in a sentence related to each other. It functions as a single unit. But it does not have a Subject (Noun) or a predicate (or verb). Each word of a phrase has meaning but it does not give complete meaning.

A Clause is also a group of words in a sentence. But it differs from phrase. A Clause has a Subject (Noun) and a Predicate (or verb). It gives complete meaning and it can even be a complete sentence. It functions as a member of a complex or compound sentence.

Example: **As soon as the bell rings,** the students came out of the class.

2. Independent / Dependent Clauses:

There are two kinds of Clauses.

    i.   Independent Clause:

        Some clauses are independent and they express a complete thought. An independent clause is a complete sentence. **Another name for independent clause is Main clause.**

Examples of Independent or Main clause:

1. The lights are not switched on. (independent or main clause)

2. Put it on the shelf. (independent or main clause-understood subject "you)

3. Since the jar fell on the floor, I called my mother. (independent or main clause)

ii.   **Dependent Clause:**

Some clauses are dependent and they cannot stand alone. They have a subject and a verb, but they do not express a complete thought. **Another name for dependent clause is Subordinate clause.**

Examples of Dependent or Subordinate Clause:

1.   When I get home, my parents are waiting for me. (dependent or subordinate clause)

2.   If you wake up early, you can see sun rise. (dependent or subordinate clause)

3.   Since the jar fell on the floor, I called my mother. (dependent or subordinate clause)

Adding the dependent marker 'Since" before the main clause "The jar fell on the floor", makes the independent clause, a dependent clause.

Some   common   dependent   markers: after, although, as, as if, because, before, even if, even though, if, in order to, since, though, unless, until, whatever, when, whenever, whether, while.

Exercise 1

Identify whether the boldened words are Main clause or Subordinate clause:

1.   **Though she is hungry,** she shares her food with the child. – Subordinate Clause

2.   When you go to the store, **get me some milk**. – Main clause

3.   The door is opened **when I entered the room.**

4.   **Till you achieve your goal**, don't stop your effort.

5.   As I need a cup of coffee, **I am heading to the restaurant**.

6.   If you plan in advance, **you will complete it well in time.**

3. Types of Clauses

The types of clauses are Noun clause, Adjective Clauses and Adverb Clauses

i.   Noun Clause

A Noun Clause is a group of words which has a subject and a predicate of its own, and does the work of a Noun.

Noun clauses often include one of the "wh-" words, such as "who," "what," "when," "where," and "why," and the related words "whatever," "whenever," and "whomever." Other question words such as "if," "how," and "that" are also common in noun clauses.

Example

- I don't understand **what you're talking about**.
- Tom can invite **whomever he chooses**.
- I believe **that I will pass the test.**

Since the noun clause does the work of a noun, it can be -

- The subject of a verb
- The object of a transitive verb
- The object of a preposition.
- The complement of a verb.

1. The Subject of a Verb

Example: Whether it will rain today, is not certain.

What Megan wrote surprised her family.

2. The Object of a Transitive Verb

Example: Let me know if the doctor is in.

He didn't know why the stove wasn't working.

3. The object of a Preposition

Example: He laughed at what the boys were saying.

Jose is not responsible for what Alex decided to do.

4. **The Complement to a Verb**

Example: Life is what we make of it.

Her excuse for being late was that she forgot to set her alarm.

Exercise 2

Replace the word in italics with suitable noun clauses:

1. He predicts *a change in the weather.*   Answer: He predicts that the weather will change.

2. He speaks *about his intelligence.*   Answer: He speaks that............

3. I heard *of your success.*   Answer: I heard that ....

4. The College President acquainted the freshers <u>with mode of opening a bank account for scholarships.</u>   Answer: The college president told the freshers how to ......

5. They asked *my help.*   Answer: They asked me if ....

Exercise 3

Complete the following sentences by adding suitable noun clauses.

1. I cannot understand ....

    Answer: I cannot understand **why she is angry with me.**

2. They said ....   Answer:

3. I think ....   Answer:

4. He told me .... Answer:

5. .... hurts me. Answer:

2. **Adjective Clause**

A group of words which has a subject and a predicate of its own, and does the work of an adjective is an adjective clause. It tells **which one** or **what kind**. Adjective clauses almost come right after the nouns they modify.

Example:

- The mug **with the stains** is his.

- The mug **which has stains** is his.

The first group of words, "with the stains" describes the coffee mug: it qualifies the noun "cup" and does the work of an adjective. It is an adjective phrase

The second group of words, "which has stains" also describes the mug and does the work of an Adjective; but because it has a subject and predicate of its own, it is called an adjective clause.

i.   **An adjective clause is introduced by a relative pronoun or by a relative adverb as in:**

Example:

- Have you seen the book I lost?

  Have you seen the book [that] I lost?

- The teacher I had in fifth grade really inspired me.

  The teacher [whom] I had in fifth grade really inspired me.

ii. **The Relative Pronoun or the Relative Adverb is sometimes not expressed in an adjective clause;** as

This is the lady, I met yesterday

(Here the relative pronoun 'whom/that' is understood)

The plan you suggest suits us.

(Here the relative pronoun 'that' is understood)

Exercise 4

Pick out the Adjective Clauses:

1.   The reason why he resigned is not known.

2.   The book that I borrowed is lost.

3.   The house where the accident took place is near the traffic signal.

4.   God helps those who help themselves.

5.   People who live in glass houses should not throw stones.

Exercise 5

Replace the Adjective Clauses by Adjectives or Adjective Phrase:

1.   I met a boy whose hair is ginger.   Answer: I met a boy with gingered hair.

2.   The dress that I wore was long and beautiful.   Answer:

3.   The day when we will receive our degrees is drawing near. Answer:

4.   The reason why Smitha failed is obvious. Answer:

5.   My father disliked the boy whose score was very poor. Answer:

3.   Adverb Clause

An adverb clause is a group of words which has a subject and a predicate of its own, and does the work of an adverb.

Example: They left **at daybreak.**

They left **when it was daybreak**.

(Both sentences speak of "when" they left)

The words in italics in the first sentence are an adverb phrase and those in the second are an adverb clause. Both the groups of words do the work of an adverb by modifying the verb "left".

And adverb clause is used as an adverb to tell us how, when, where, why, how much or under what conditions something happens or takes place.

i.   Kinds of Adverb Clauses

An adverb clause does the work of an adverb. It can be of the following kinds:

Time	Result or Consequence
Place	Comparison
Manner	Condition
Cause or Reason	Supposition or Concession
Purpose	

1. **Adverb Clauses of Time** - Adverb Clauses of Time are introduced by subordinating conjunctions like - when, whenever, since, before, after, till, as.

   - Before you leave, kindly meet me.

   - As soon as I heard the news, I rushed to the spot.

2. **Adverb Clauses of Place** - Adverb clauses of place are introduced by subordinating conjunctions like where, wherever, whence.

   - The puppy followed the boy wherever he went.

   - Where the eagles soar, no bird can reach.

3. **Adverb Clauses of Manner** - Adverb clauses of manner are introduced by subordinating conjunctions like as, if, as if, though

   - As you sow, so shall you reap.

   - The cat sprang off the wall as if it had seen a ghost.

4. **Adverb Clauses of Cause or Reason** - Adverb clauses of cause or reason are introduced by subordinating conjunctions like - because, since, that, as

   - The child was frightened because it was lonely.

   - As he was absent, we couldn't meet him.

5. **Adverb Clauses of Purpose** - Adverb clauses of purpose are introduced by subordinating conjunctions like that, in order that, so that, lest.

   - Work hard that you may succeed in your game.

   - Take care so that you don't lose the data.

6. **Adverb clauses of Result or Consequence** - Adverb clauses of result or consequence are introduced by subordinating conjunctions like that (normally preceded by 'so' or 'such' in the main clause). Sometimes, the conjunction is understood:

   - He ran so fast that he was terribly out of breath.

   - The foreigner spoke with such a thick accent that nobody understood him.

7. **Adverb clauses of Comparison** - Adverb clauses of comparison of degree are introduced by one of the subordinating conjunctions, or relative adverbs like – as, then

   - She is as beautiful as she is beautiful.

   - He is not as foolish as you take him to be.

8. **Adverb clauses of Condition** - Adverb clauses of condition are generally introduced by subordinating conjunctions

   - If it rains, the pitch will be spoilt.

   - I must do my best whether I like it or not.

9. **Adverb clauses of Supposition or Connection** - Adverb clauses of supposition or concession are introduced by subordinating conjunctions like - although, though

   - He is successful though he doesn't work hard

   - Although it was a holiday, he went to his office.

Exercise 6

Underline the adverb clauses in the following sentences:

1. We must get some vinegar so that we can prepare pickle

2. Place your bag where you can locate it

3. When we were young, we used to cycle all over town

4. She talks as if everything can change overnight.

Exercise 7

Replace the adverb phrase with an adverb clause:

1. Linda likes to wear colourful clothes.

2. Tom is a careful driver.

3. I wish to go for a vacation.

4. This is a game to be played with another person.

Exercise 8

Replace the Adverb Clause with an Adverb or Adverb Phrase:

1. The heat was so scorching that people walking barefoot suffered.

2. When she sees a cockroach, she runs away.

3. As it was raining heavily, we didn't go out.

4. Good writers choose information that is important for their topic.

References:

Bhatnagar. R.P. 2009. *English for Competitive Examinations* (3rd Edition). Department of English, University of Rajasthan, Jaipur. Macmillan Publishers India Ltd., ISBN:9780230-638075. pp.357-360.

Kumar, R.Kishore, Julu Sen, and R.Lalitha Eapen. 2012. *Methods of Teaching English* – Block III: Units 2 to 5, *Skills in Language Learning and Use* (PGCTE Course Material). Hyderabad: The English and Foreign Languages University.

Dobson, M.Julia. 2003. *Dialogues for Everyday Use*. Washington: Office of English Language Programs, Bureau of Educational and Cultural Affairs, United States Department of State. DC 20547 (https://exchanges.state.gov/education?engteaching/).

Murphy, Raymond. 2005. *Intermediate English Grammar*. Cambridge University Press.

Nair, Bhaskaran, P. 2018. *Functioning in English* (A Multi-skill Language Course for Undergraduate Programmes) Book 1 (Semester 1). ISBN: 978-81-7966-174-1. Chennai: Emerald Publishers.

Peterson, Patricia Wilcox. 2003. *Developing Writing*. Writing Skills Practice Book for EFL. Washington: Office of English Language Programs, Bureau of Educational and Cultural Affairs, United States Department of State. DC 20547

(https://exchanges.state.gov/education?engteaching/).

Santhi, V.Jeya and Selvam R, *Advanced Skills for Communication in English: Book I*, ISBN:978-81-2343-101-7. Chennai: New Century Book House. December 2015 (Pages 176).

https://7esl.com/english-collocations/

https://www.collopedia.com/post/strong-fixed-and-weak-collocations

https://www.ecenglish.com/learnenglish/lessons/collocations-learn-correct-english

https://www.englishgrammar101.com/module-10/clauses/lesson-2/adjective-clauses

https://www.englishgrammar.org/noun-clause-exercise-2/

https://www.englishlessonviaskype.com/english-collocations-with-time/

https://hrmpractice.com/what-is-a-formal-interview-2/

https://icebreakerideas.com/skit-ideas/#Skits_for_College_Students

https://www.indeed.com › Career Guide › Interviewing

https://www.iudehradun.edu.in/IUEVENTS/Skit-on-Social-Issues.pdf

https://www.moravian.edu › basic-interview-formats

https://www.myprimaryparadise.com/2021/03/12/readers-theater/

https://www.readingrockets.org/strategies/readers_theater

https://skillsforchange.com/what-is-a-formal-interview/

https://studycorgi.com/stages-of-formal-and-informal-interviews/.
Education Words: 802 Pages: 2 Jan 17th, 2022

https://totempool.com/blog/formal-informal-interview/

https://en.wikipedia.org › wiki › Interview

https://youtu.be/PGbPiIxhzw4

References

Nair, B (2018). *Functioning in English*, Emerald Publishers, Chennai.

Tayfoor, S (2004). Common Mistakes at Upper Intermediate Level, Cambridge University, Press, New Delhi.

Wren W (2016). My English Folder- An Innovative Approach to Learning, Oxford University Press, New Delhi.

https://www.english-grammar-today.com/a-preposition.html

https://www.cambridgeenglish.org/images/vocabulary-games-and-activities.pdf

https://www.eenglishgrammar.com/2020/08/lesson-plan-of-adverbs.html

https://education.missouri.edu/wp-content/uploads/sites/21/2012/10/Vocabulary-Lesson-Classroom-Ideas.pdf

https://www.thoughtco.com/what-is-active-vocabulary-1689060

https://blog.talk.edu/learn-english/12-fun-english-vocabulary-facts/

https://uwaterloo.ca/centre-for-teaching-excellence/teaching-resources/teaching-tips/developing-assignments/group-work/group-work-classroom-types-small-groups

https://www.advance-africa.com/all-that-glitters-is-not-gold.html

http://blog.tesol.org/using-proverbs-in-a-writing-class/

https://www.fluentu.com/blog/educator-english/intonation-activities-teaching-english/

https://www.teachingenglish.org.uk/sites/teacheng/files/TeachingSpeaking_4_stressintonation_v01.pdf

https://courses.lumenlearning.com/suny jeffersoncc-introliterature/chapter/stress-in-poetry/

https://www.twinkl.co.in/teaching-wiki/intonation

https://usefulenglish.ru/phonetics/rising-intonation

https://www.tweetspeakpoetry.com/2015/10/23/5-great-tips-for-reading-poetry-aloud/

https://bihar-cetbed-lnmu.in/welcome-speech-in-english/

https://gupshups.org/vote-of-thanks/

https://saylordotorg.github.io/text_stand-up-speak-out-the-practice-and-ethics-of-public-speaking/s17-delivering-the-speech.html

Koneru, A (2011) English Language Skills, Tata McGraw-Hill, New Delhi.

https://emile-education.com/conjunctions/

https://www.easyteacherworksheets.com/pages/pdf/languagearts/partsofspeech/interjection/2.html

(https://www.kidsworldfun.com/learn-english/interjections.php)

https://www.yourdictionary.com/index.php/pdf/articles/315.interjections-worksheet.pdf

Santhi, V. Jeya, and R.Selvam. 2015. Advanced Skills for Communication in English: Book I, ISBN:978-81-2343-101-7. Chennai: New Century Book House.